TRUE STORIES OF
POLAR
ADVENTURES

This edition first published in 2015 by Usborne Publishing Ltd,
Usborne House, 83-85 Saffron Hill,
London EC1N 8RT, England.
www.usborne.com

Copyright © 2015, 2007, 2002 Usborne Publishing Ltd.
U.E. First published in America in 2015.

A catalogue record for this title is available
from the British Library.

Printed in Great Britain

Series editors: Jane Chisholm, Jenny Tyler and Rosie Dickins
Designer: Brian Voakes
Series designer: Mary Cartwright
Illustrator: John Woodcock
Cover designer: Amy Manning
Cover image © Bridgeman Images, Alamy Images

With grateful thanks to Fergus Fleming, and Robert Headland,
Archivist and Museum Curator at the Scott Polar Research Institute,
Cambridge, for their extremely helpful comments on the manuscript.
Thanks also to Shirley Sawtell of the Scott Polar Institute Library,
and Sir Ranulph Fiennes and Dr. Mike Stroud, who kindly read and
commented on their story.

ISBN 9781474903820
JFMAMJJ SOND/15 01873-5

TRUE STORIES OF
POLAR
ADVENTURES

CONTENTS

The top and bottom of the world

If you have a globe, spin it around. The two places where your globe is anchored to its frame are the North and South Poles – the top and bottom of the world – once thought to be as unreachable as distant planets. What an explorer would actually find at these two spots provoked feverish speculation right up until the early 20th century. Would they provide an entrance into new worlds inside our planet? What strange creatures might live in such inhospitable surroundings? Perhaps the North or South Pole might be the location of the Garden of Eden?

But the Poles are only the creation of human mathematics – just positions on a map marked by a reading of 90° degrees north or 90° degrees south, based on a system of map coordinates known as latitude and longitude.* As actual places, they are

---

*Latitude gives the location of a place north or south of the equator, with 0° being the equator, and 90° north or south being the furthest point away from the equator. Longitude gives the location of places east and west of a central 0° line, which runs through Greenwich in London. For greater accuracy, these degrees are also divided further into measurements of 60 "minutes", with each minute being divided into 60 "seconds". By giving map references in degrees, minutes and seconds, it is possible to locate any spot on earth with great precision.

remarkably unremarkable. Explorer Robert Falcon Scott noted with some disappointment, when he got to the South Pole in 1912, that there was "very little that is different from the awful monotony of past days".

These days, explorers carry GPS (Global Positioning System) navigation tools. These extraordinary little electronic devices use a network of 24 satellites to take an exact reading of their position anywhere on earth. Before the invention of these devices in the 1990s, navigators used compasses to determine which direction they were facing, and sextants to establish their latitude or longitude. (An essential seafarer's tool, a sextant looks like a big wooden triangle; it works by comparing the position of the sun or a particular star with the horizon, at a set time.)

The Arctic (see map opposite) is a huge frozen ocean around the North Pole, surrounded by an intricate mosaic of bleak islands – especially off its Canadian shore. In the days before whole continents and oceans could be captured in a single satellite photograph, it proved fatally difficult to chart and explore. Although the Arctic has been visited by European traders and settlers for more than 1,000 years, it wasn't until the last century that a detailed map of its icy core was completed.

The first serious attempts to explore the Arctic were prompted by the need to discover a sea route

Map of the North Pole

from Europe to China and other Far Eastern countries. There were two basic ways around: northeast above the coast of Russia, or northwest through the Canadaian Arctic. Here, Europeans came into contact with the *Inuit*, the inhabitants of the Arctic (also sometimes referred to as Eskimos). In

9

their arrogance, many early explorers dismissed the Inuit as Stone Age savages, but their ability to survive in such a barren, inhospitable region showed great ingenuity.

The initial exploration of the regions north of Russia and continental Canada was tortuously slow and exceptionally dangerous. In 1553, English seafarer Sir Hugh Willoughby led an expedition of three ships off the Siberian coast, in search of the northeast passage. Willoughby died and two of his ships were lost.

In 1594, Dutchman Willem Barents made another epic voyage from Russia into the Arctic Ocean. He reached Novaya Zemlya – a pair of islands the length of the United Kingdom, which point from the coast of Siberia deep into the Arctic Ocean. Trapped there when ice destroyed their ship, his crew built a house from the remains of the ship to keep them alive in the cruel Arctic winter. The following spring, they sailed two small boats back to the Russian mainland. Barents died during the voyage, but the sea northwest of Novaya Zemlya was named after him.

In 1610, Henry Hudson set out to North America to explore the northwest passage. A mutiny left him stranded, and he died in a small boat in the polar wastes with his 16-year-old son and eight loyal members of his crew. The mutineers sailed the ship back to England, where they were treated with surprising leniency. Sailors with such vital knowledge of unknown lands were too valuable to string up on the yardarm of a ship.

From 1733 to 1743, the Russian Admiralty mounted a "Great Northern Expedition" to chart the Arctic coasts of Siberia. Facing extreme hardship, seven parties, numbering 977 men in all, succeeded in charting the entire Arctic coast of Russia, from the Atlantic to the Pacific.

At that time, however, the Arctic coast of Canada west of the Hudson Bay was virtually unknown. This was to change in the first half of the 19th century, when British explorers made repeated efforts to open up the northwest passage. These efforts culminated in Sir John Franklin's expedition of 1845-1848. The journey was a disaster; his ships were lost and all his crew died. But, over the next 10 years, 40 expeditions were launched to find him. In the course of their travels they surveyed their surroundings, which contributed greatly to the mapping of this fiendishly complex region.

The discovery and exploration of Antarctica, the continent where the South Pole is located (see map on next page), was simpler, as it is not surrounded by such a complicated maze of islands. Nonetheless, it was only sighted for the first time in 1820 – although explorers had guessed there was an "uninhabited land" to the far south for a couple of hundred years before this. Antarctica is a vast continent, twice the size of Australia. In places, land lies beneath a layer of ice 4km (2½ miles) deep.

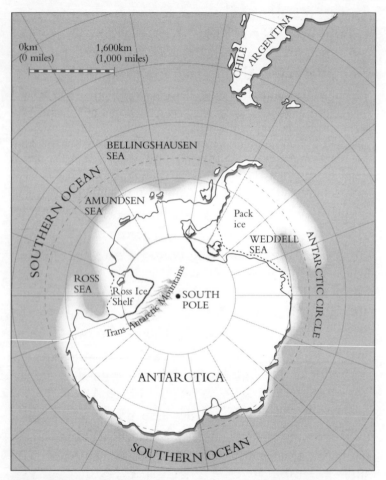

Map of the South Pole

The great age of polar exploration occurred in the decades before the First World War. In the Arctic, by this time, the complexities of the northeast and northwest passage were much more clearly understood, and adventurers were advancing steadily towards the top of the world. In the Antarctic, seafarers felt more confident they could build ships strong enough to withstand the crushing ice fields that surround the continent – although their confidence was sometimes misplaced. It is still less than a century since both poles were first visited by humans. In those days, radio and aircraft were such new inventions that their use was barely considered. Instead, it was the fate of the polar explorer to spend months at sea before reaching these unknown lands. Once there, they ventured into them in the certain knowledge that, if anything went wrong, they would be beyond rescue.

So many things could go wrong, it was astounding that anyone went at all. The cold was incessant, and pierced men to the bone. Even the strongest ships could be caught in pack ice and crushed to matchsticks. At the top and bottom of the world, midsummer and midwinter are marked by days of constant light or dark. In the polar winter, the endless darkness drove men insane. Lack of a proper diet, especially food containing vitamin C, led to scurvy. This horrible disorder, known among all seafarers until the 20th century, takes its name from an old English word for "gnawing". An exhausted sailor battling with the disease feels he is being eaten away from the inside by its hideous symptoms. His gums turn black and recede until his teeth drop out. His arms and legs swell up, and his joints ache, so that every movement is a trial. His skin is covered with livid rashes and ulcers, which ooze blood and pus. Scurvy attacks the body's weakest points. Fresh wounds never heal. Old wounds, long since healed, open up again, to add to the torments inflicted by the condition. Early in the 20th century, scurvy still occurred, and was still fairly misunderstood. Captain Scott's famous expedition, for example, was fatally hindered by the disease.

Along with scurvy, men also suffered from frostbite. Here, body tissues in the most exposed parts of the body, such as the hands, toes, noses and ears, freeze, preventing blood from reaching them. Deprived of its normal blood supply, the skin and flesh of these parts dies. When the affected area thaws, the victim suffers extreme pain. Left untreated, frostbite can turn to gangrene, where the flesh rots, poisoning the whole body. Frostbite remains one of the greatest threats to explorers of both poles. It affected such modern-day explorers as Børge Ousland, in 2001, just as surely as it blighted Sir Hugh Willoughby's expedition in 1553.

Today, if you have the time and the money, you can book a vacation which will take you to the North or South Pole. Here, you can stand on the exact spot before hopping aboard a warm plane or icebreaker which will take you back to civilization in a matter of hours. One travel company even drops clients off at 89° north or south, and they ski the final degree, to be met by a plane for the return journey. In 2002, one pilot made an emergency landing on an Arctic icefloe off the coast of Greenland. Not only did he use his mobile phone to summon help, but he even managed to transmit to his rescuers images of his surroundings, taken with a digital camera, to give them a clearer idea of where he could be found.

But these comfortable tales of hi-tech adventure are not typical of the experience of most polar explorers. Almost a century ago, British explorer Apsley Cherry-Garrard famously said: "Polar exploration is at once the cleanest, most isolated way of having a bad time which has ever been devised" – as you'll find out in the stories in this book...

The *Polaris* mystery

How Charles Hall's wife must have regretted the day he ever picked up a book about Sir John Franklin and his lost expedition. The story was to spark an interest in the Arctic that would frequently take her husband away on long expeditions, and eventually leave her an almost penniless widow, with a 10-year-old son who had barely met his father.

Hall's interest in Franklin was further stoked when he went to hear Lady Franklin speak about her ill-fated explorer husband, in the Halls' home town of Cincinnati, in 1849. Eleven years later, in 1860, Hall had managed to raise enough money to embark on a two-year exploration of the southeast coast of Baffin Island. Here, he searched unsuccessfully for any clue to Franklin's demise.

Hall was not an adventurer by profession. He made his living as a newspaper publisher. The only known photograph of him shows an intense, heavily built, dark-haired man, with a huge, bushy beard. He had a deeply-held Christian faith, and the Arctic sent him into a state of religious ecstasy. On observing the Northern Lights, also known as the *Aurora Borealis*, he recorded: "*It seemeth to me as if the very doors of heaven have been opened tonight, so mighty and beauteous and marvellous were the waves of golden light.*"

While on his exploratory trip to Baffin Island, he met an Inuit couple named Tookolito and Ebierbing, who had been taken to London in the 1850s by a British whaling captain. Here, they had learned to speak English, and had adopted the manners and fashions of polite English society. They were a sensation in both Britain and the United States. Eventually, when people tired of this novelty, the pair were returned to Baffin Island. But they would feature heavily in Hall's unfortunate future, as would Sidney Budington, the captain of the ship that first took him north.

Two years after his Baffin Island trip, Hall set off on another epic expedition in search of Franklin. This time, he was away for five years, and returned with a few relics left behind by a previous British expedition – mainly sacks of coal. But what Hall really wanted to do was travel to the North Pole. Over the years, this ambition grew into an obsession. He was, he declared, "born to discover the North Pole. Once I have set my right foot on the Pole I shall be perfectly willing to die." (Mrs. Hall and their son obviously inspired no great feeling of responsibility.)

Like all explorers, of course, he needed money to get there. It was now several years since Tookolito and Ebierbing had visited the United States. So, to raise funds, he brought the Inuit couple over for a lecture tour. While Hall talked about the mysterious Arctic, they were exhibited alongside seal-skin clothing and boats known as kayaks. He even leased them to P.T.

Barnum's infamous circus of freaks and curiosities.

Eventually, though, his fund-raising efforts proved unnecessary. In 1870, Hall managed to persuade the US government to back him. He was given a Navy tug, the *Periwinkle*, which he promptly renamed the *Polaris* – another name for the North Star, which lies almost directly above the North Pole. $50,000 was spent strengthening the tug's bow, which transformed it into a formidable Arctic vessel, strong enough to withstand the ice and storms it would have to face.

No polar explorer could have hoped for a better ship. But in choosing its crew, Hall seriously hindered his chances of success. The extreme conditions and dangers of polar exploration in the 19th century called for men with a special kind of spirit – team players with a combination of boundless optimism and common decency. Alas, these were qualities that most of Hall's companions lacked to an alarming extent.

First of all, Hall picked his old Arctic companion Sidney Budington. But this once-respected whaling captain was now a secret drinker. Furthermore, he had no great respect for Hall, and no interest at all in reaching the Pole. Still, he must have thought, a job is a job. Hall, who was mainly used to working on his own, had no experience of commanding an expedition. As if to compensate for this, he hired two other former sea captains as senior officers on the ship: Hubbard Chester was taken on as first mate, and George Tyson was to be assistant navigator. Tyson, as it turned out, would be the hero of the sorry story that followed.

In order to secure US government help, Hall had agreed to bring several scientists along, to keep records and collect rock, plant and animal specimens. Chief among the scientists was a respected but forbidding German academic and surgeon, Dr. Emil Bessels. Another German, Frederick Meyer, was the expedition meteorologist. Hall resented having the scientists on board, fearing that their work would interfere with his own ambition to reach the Pole. The crew included Tookolito, Ebierbing and their young son, and a large number of German sailors. And, when the *Polaris* stopped off in Greenland, they were joined by another Inuit couple with their three children.

The *Polaris* sailed from New York in July 1871. Just before departure, Hall declared their future would be "glorious". George Tyson's own view of the expedition, recorded in his journal a week after the voyage began, was to be much more prophetic: "*I see there is not perfect harmony between Captain Hall and the Scientific Corp, nor with some others either. I am afraid things will not work well.*"

Hall's inexperience as a leader of men showed at every turn. Almost immediately he fell out with the scientists, and with Budington, who would raid the storeroom for medicinal alcohol to feed his addiction. (This alcohol was intended for use as an antiseptic, and also as a preservative for animal specimens.) Budington, Chester and Tyson, all experienced sea captains, saw each other as rivals. The Germans, Americans and Inuit formed their own cliques, rarely mixing with each other.

Yet, despite the sometimes heated arguments and open animosity, the voyage of the *Polaris* was quite a success. Good weather ensured remarkable progress. By August 29, the ship had passed through Smith Sound into the narrow channel that separates the north west coast of Greenland from Ellesmere Island. Here, existing navigation charts came to an end, and they began to map out virgin territory. In early September, the *Polaris* reached 82°. Ahead lay a clear sea, and the promise of more fine weather. But Budington had gone as far north as he was prepared to go. His years of experience told him that the further they went, the more difficult it would be to get back.

Autumn was approaching. The crew settled in a bay in the newly named territory of Hall Land, in northern Greenland, to wait out the winter. Hall called their berth "Thank God Harbor". When they were settled, and ice had frozen around their ship, Hall gave his men a grateful pep talk. He eloquently summed up the sacrifices they had made and the quest they had undertaken: "You have left your homes, friends, and country; indeed, you have bid a long farewell for a time to the whole civilized world, for the purpose of aiding me in discovering the mysterious, hidden parts of the earth." When the spring came, he told them, they would head north again.

So far, Hall had been lucky. His fractious and divided crew had worked well together so long as there had been good weather, they were reasonably warm and well fed, and there was plenty to keep them occupied. The coming months, when they would be stuck in bleak, monotonous surroundings, with dark winter nights, blizzards and gales, would test them all to the limit.

Sure enough, before the year was out, disaster struck. Hall had never been a particularly healthy man, and previous Arctic expeditions had taken their toll. The first clear sign of his demise came in October. On an exploratory sled trip with a team of dogs, Hall forgot to pack several vital pieces of equipment. A companion had to be sent back to the *Polaris* to fetch warm winter clothing, a stove and a chronometer (which they would need to find their way back to the ship). Hall's mind was obviously failing him fast.

When Hall returned two weeks later, he complained about his inability to keep up with the dogs, meaning he had often had to ride on the sled. Physical as well as mental weakness was overtaking him. Then, as soon as he came aboard and drank a warming cup of coffee, he was violently sick. His decline thereafter was steady and certain. Confined to his bed, he became delirious and began to accuse his companions of poisoning him.

In early November, Hall seemed to make a startling recovery, and raised himself from his bed to work on his journal. But all was clearly not well. He was distracted, and would lose track of what he was saying. Paralysis set in, and his eyes took on a doomed, glassy appearance. He slipped into unconsciousness, and died on November 8, 1871. He was buried close to the ship in the cold, pebble ground of Thank God Harbor.

His death is a mystery to this day. He could have suffered a stroke, or a heart attack – both ailments present symptoms similar to those described by Hall's companions. But he could also have been poisoned. Arsenic produces similar effects to both these illnesses. In the 1960s, a biographer of Hall's asked for permission to visit the grave and examine the body. Hall was duly exhumed and found to be fairly well preserved (as bodies generally are in such a cold environment). Samples of hair and fingernails were removed and sent to a forensic laboratory in Montreal, which specialized in the examination of long-dead bodies. Tests showed conclusively that Hall had ingested a large quantity of arsenic. But had he been murdered?

There are several arguments for and against this. Given the acrimonious relations between Hall, his captain and the scientists, it is possible that one of them decided to kill him. Bessels, as a doctor, was a prime suspect. Perhaps he thought they would be free to carry out their work more efficiently with Hall out of the way. Budington, too, might have poisoned Hall, because he did not wish to take the ship any further north.

But arsenic, in small doses, was a common medicine in the late 19th century. It was a standard ingredient in remedies for indigestion, from which Hall regularly suffered. Perhaps Hall suffered a heart attack or massive stroke, and trusting no one, tried to treat himself from his own medicine supply, accidentally giving himself an overdose of arsenic. Perhaps he was poisoned deliberately. We shall never know.

With Hall gone, control of the expedition passed to Captain Budington, who had already made it clear to everyone that he thought the whole trip was a waste of time. Taking command did not change his view. The morale of the already divided crew sank dramatically.

Before he died, Hall had made some successful efforts at uniting his crew. For example, a regular Sunday service had been established, but this was now abandoned. As well as providing an opportunity for all the crew to come together, the service had been a weekly ritual that marked the passage of time. Now the crew's winter existence became formless, and the days and weeks slipped into an unmarked void. Budington made other, seemingly bizarre, decisions. The whole crew was issued with firearms, the idea being that if any animal came by – a stray bird or a lone seal – it could be shot whenever the chance arose. But the prospect of a fractious, divided crew, all carrying weapons, was alarming.

The atmosphere on the *Polaris* plummeted further when some of the crew broke into the scientists' supply of alcohol. Officers and men would terrorize the ship in drunken rampages. It was difficult enough getting by in the endless polar winter, but now everyone's nerves were in tatters. The ship's carpenter, Nathaniel Coffin, went insane. Convinced the rest of the crew was trying to murder him in the most gruesome ways, he would never sleep in the same spot. Instead, he wandered around the decks and passageways of the *Polaris*, muttering and raving according to his mood.

Winter passed, but spring brought no thaw in the ice surrounding the ship, although wildlife was now more plentiful and there was no danger of starvation. By midsummer, there was still no sign that the ice would crack and allow them to escape.

Then, on August 12, 1872, two events occurred to brighten their dreary existence. One of the Inuit women, who had come aboard at Greenland, gave birth to a baby. This was a total surprise to everyone except her and her husband, as her swollen belly had been concealed by her bulky, seal-skin clothing. The baby was named Charles Polaris, after the dead commander and his ship. On that same day, the ice broke up, and the *Polaris* set out to sea after nearly a year at Thank God Harbor. But their luck did not last. Within three days they were stuck fast in pack ice once again, but at least this ice was slowly drifting south.

As the nights grew longer and the supply of wildlife to hunt grew sparser, the crew had to accept that they were in for another Arctic winter. By now, the *Polaris* was leaking badly, and tons of precious coal were being used to keep the ship's pumps working to clear the hold of seawater. An argument between Budington and members of his crew, over whether they should pump water by hand to save coal, ended with a cabin door being slammed in his face. And these tensions were to grow worse. Much worse.

On October 15, during a terrible storm, the ice around the *Polaris* was hit by a huge iceberg, dramatically increasing the pressure on the hull. The ship's engineer ran up onto the deck, shouting that water was pouring into the hold. In the panic that followed, Budington ordered two lifeboats and some crates of supplies to be lowered overboard onto the ice. But, after four hours, the *Polaris* seemed to be no lower in the water than she had been before the iceberg had struck. It had been a false alarm.

George Tyson was on the ice, helping to supervise the unloading of the ship. He and Captain Budington had a heated shouting match from ship to ice, about whether to load the boats and supplies back onto the *Polaris*. Budington, strangely, ordered the men on the ice to move these items even further away from the ship. While Tyson pondered this peculiar order, the ice surrounding the ship began to crack. As the snow whirled around their heads, and the wind tossed the sea into a swirling inferno, the men on the ice watched the *Polaris* drift beyond their reach and vanish into the dark night.

Morning came and the storm passed. The 19 members of the *Polaris* stranded on the ice now had the chance to examine their new home. In other circumstances they might have been charmed by their surroundings. The floe was like a miniature island. There were lakes of fresh water, formed by melted snow, and little hillocks. Altogether, the ice measured about 6km (4 miles) in circumference.

Tyson, as the most senior officer, was supposedly in command. He faced an impossible task. His fellow castaways, already a divided bunch, would be driven even further apart by their desperate circumstances. Aboard the *Polaris*, when it had lurched away from the ice, had been Budington, Bessels and 12 of the crew. Here on the floe, Tyson had Frederick Meyer, most of the Germans, the two Inuit couples and their five children, including baby Charles. The Germans seemed to regard Meyer as their leader, but his authority was fragile. To make matters worse, he had little respect for Tyson.

That first day, a large chunk of ice broke off, carrying one of the boats, several bags of biscuits and their only compass – although in an amazing stroke of good fortune, the chunk of ice floated back to them a week later. The castaways set up two separate camps. The Germans put up tents in their own little community. The Inuit built igloos, and Tyson and the other crewmen joined them.

In circumstances such as these, people stand a much better chance of survival if they work together, helping the weakest and conserving supplies. But despite his best efforts, Tyson could not get the German sailors to cooperate. They would raid his food supply, often bingeing until they were sick. They burned one of the boats to keep warm. They even stole some of his clothing. Worst of all, when their food supplies grew dangerously low and no animals could be caught, they suggested eating the Inuit children. Tyson was horrified. But, when the *Polaris* had broken away from the ice, the German sailors had been carrying their guns, and he had not. There was nothing he could do to enforce his control.

Fortunately, one group among the castaways was prepared to help them all. Starvation that winter was prevented thanks mainly to the Inuit's hunting skills. By some extraordinary miracle, no one died and no one killed anyone else. But, just as the worst seemed to be over and the survivors could begin to look forward to spring, the floe began to break up.

By the middle of March, their little world had shrunk to a mere fraction of what it had been, and it was getting smaller by the day. Then, towering icebergs surrounded them, threatening to smash the shrinking floe into ice splinters. There was nothing left to do but take to the remaining boat. Cramming 19 people into a rowing boat meant for eight wasn't easy. Having already threatened to eat the Inuit children, some of the Germans loudly suggested that the children should be thrown overboard to make more room.

The nightmare journey that followed would haunt them all for the rest of their lives. In heaving seas of ice and mountainous waves, the tiny, overloaded boat battled against the freezing wind to reach land. By night, they would stop on a floe and try to sleep. By day, they would cower in their tiny boat, weakening by the hour through lack of food and fresh water.

On April 8, when a crack unexpectedly opened on the edge of a floe they were resting on, Meyer fell into the freezing sea. Ebierbing, and another Inuit named Hans, ran out through wobbling chunks of ice to pull him out. The shock of falling into sub-zero water almost killed Meyer. He stopped breathing and would have died, had not the Inuit pummelled his body until he regained consciousness. The fall crushed his spirit, and left him frost-bitten and feverish. Recalling his appearance in the days after, Tyson wrote: "*he is very tall and thin. If [an artist] had wanted a model to stand for Famine, he might have drawn Meyer… He was the most wretched-looking object I ever saw.*" Tyson feared that Meyer's decline would bring him further trouble. Meyer had had some authority over his fellow Germans. As he grew weaker, it all but evaporated.

In their darkest hour, the men seemed to rediscover their humanity. On the evening of April 19, the castaways made camp on a floe, but then a fierce storm broke around nine o'clock, and torrents of water swamped their icy refuge. The men bundled the Inuit women and children into the boat, and then held onto their slippery perch as best they could. After each wave washed over them, they would haul the boat back into the middle and wait for the next onslaught.

In the early morning light, they could see the floe was melting into the sea, and the boat was launched. Aside from the sound of crying children, a strange silence fell over the usually mutinous crew. Stunned by their narrow escape and the horror of their circumstances, they finally looked to Tyson for leadership, and readily obeyed his every command as he attempted to steer the overcrowded boat.

In the days that followed, the weather grew worse. Of the wind and the sea, Tyson wrote in his journal: "*They played with us and our boat as if we were shuttlecocks.*" Reviewing their situation, he concluded: "*Half-drowned we are, and cold enough in our wet clothes, without shelter, and not sun enough to dry us even on the outside. We have nothing to eat; everything is finished and gone. The prospect looks bad."*

However the situation was not as bad as Tyson imagined. By now, they had drifted far enough south to have reached the usual limits of the whale and seal ships that roamed the Arctic. They sighted their first ship on the afternoon of April 28. This must have been the moment when everyone on board allowed themselves to hope that they might survive their journey after all. But fate had not finished with them yet. The first two ships they sighted did not see their frantic signals. It was only on the morning of April 30 that they were finally rescued, by a Newfoundland sealer called the *Tigress*.

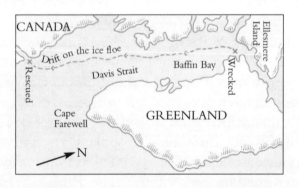

This map shows the castaways' journey to safety.

Safely back home in the United States, Tyson learned of the fate of the *Polaris*. The men on board had fared little better than those stranded on the ice floe. As the ship floated away, it had sprung a serious leak, and Budington had been forced to land on the west coast of Smith Sound. Having previously abandoned the ship's lifeboats on the ice, the crew had had to dismantle their vessel to build smaller boats. These they used to travel down the coast until they reached the whale and seal hunting grounds, and were rescued by a Scottish whaler.

When news of Hall's disastrous expedition broke, it caused a sensation and a scandal. It read, after all, like a cross between a boy's adventure story and a psychological murder mystery. The ordeal of the Inuit women and children provoked particular sympathy among American newspaper readers, and the Inuit families were inundated with gifts of bundles of clothing.

But there were also serious questions to be answered. The United States government launched an inquiry into the loss of the ship and the death of its commander. Much of the story came out, but it was difficult to piece together any clear picture among all the conflicting accounts. If any dirty deeds had been done, neither the officers nor the crew were willing to admit them. The Board of Inquiry decided that Hall had died of a stroke. Despite the discovery of arsenic traces when his body was exhumed in the 1960s, there is still no solid evidence to suggest he was murdered, and no obvious prime suspect.

Interlude

From 1873-1908

Charles Hall's disastrous failure to reach the North Pole, and the terrible hardships that befell his crew, merely whetted the appetite of other explorers to do better. In 1879, an American expedition, under the leadership of Lieutenant Commander George Washington De Long, set sail through the Bering Strait, off the coast of eastern Siberia, in the ship *Jeanette*. De Long intended to sail as far north as possible, and then use sleds to reach the Pole itself. But the ship became caught in ice and drifted for 22 months, before sinking off the coast of eastern Siberia.

When wreckage from the *Jeanette* drifted over to Greenland, Norwegian explorer Fridtjof Nansen hit on the idea of reaching the North Pole by drifting there in a strong ship. Accordingly, he set out in a ship specially designed to resist crushing by ice. The ship was called the *Fram* (which means "forward"). During the three-year journey that followed, between 1893 and 1896, Nansen and his crew gained vast amounts of knowledge about the Arctic, establishing once and for all that the North Pole was just part of a huge icy sea, rather than solid land. At one point on the journey, Nansen and a colleague left the *Fram* intending to sled and ski their way to the North Pole. They failed, and were forced to spend the winter on Franz Josef Island, until they were rescued by a British explorer.

At the turn of the century, American, German, Swedish and Italian teams all crept closer to the Pole, and it seemed only a matter of time before someone would stand at that elusive point where their navigational instruments would read 90° North.

Over in the Antarctic, an international team aboard the Belgian ship *Belgica* was trapped in ice in the Bellinghausen Sea. Between 1898 and 1899, they became the first people to winter south of the Antarctic Circle. A year later, a British expedition under Carsten E. Borchgrevink spent the winter on the continent itself, at Cape Adare.

It was the British who made the greatest progress exploring the Antarctic. In two expeditions, from 1901–1904, and again from 1907–1909, Captain Robert Falcon Scott and Sir Ernest Shackleton both led sled parties deep into the heart of Antarctica. Scott and Shackleton became rivals, and it seemed certain that one of them would be the first explorer to reach the South Pole.

"Won at last by the Stars and Stripes"

More often than not, success is not half as interesting as failure. When the North Pole was finally conquered, the story of the first team to reach this anonymous spot on the map was notably lacking in drama – aside from the murder of one of the party by his Inuit companion. It was what happened afterwards that proved to be far more interesting.

The man popularly credited as being the first to the North Pole was US Navy engineer Robert Peary. At the start of the century, he was already the most eminent Arctic explorer of his age. He was a tall, wiry man, with a huge walrus moustache. In almost all his photographs he stares out at the world with haughty disdain. A lifetime dedicated to reaching the North Pole had turned Robert Peary into a rather objectionable human being. Yet, from such arrogance and self-belief, heroes are often made.

Despite his disagreeable personality, there were some qualities, at least, to admire in Peary. He was a person of great contradictions. As a white man, he regarded himself as superior to other races. (This prejudice was commonplace at the time.) Yet he had a black servant, Matthew Henson, who was both his right hand man and loyal companion. Peary repaid this loyalty by taking Henson with him on the first trip to the Pole. (Although his detractors say this was because he did not want to share the glory of being first with another white man.)

The Inuit, then known as Eskimos, he also saw as an inferior race. But he admired their ability to survive in their barren, frozen environment, and learned a great deal from them. This was not true of all explorers. For example, many British explorers were highly sceptical that they could learn anything from a people they regarded as savages, and suffered as a consequence. For his time, Peary had a commendable respect for the Inuit. When asked whether attempts should be made to convert them to Christianity, Peary was certain they should be left to their own religious beliefs. After all, he remarked, "the cardinal graces of faith, hope and charity they seem to have already. They are healthy and pure-blooded; they have no vices, no intoxicants and no bad habits, not even gambling."

Peary's accounts of his trips make much of the hardship of polar exploration. One passage describes his feet feeling "*hot, aching, and throbbing, till the pain reached to my knees*". His own courage could not be doubted. During an Arctic expedition in 1898, he lost nine toes to gangrene brought on by frostbite. Thereafter, he walked with a curious sliding gait. But even this didn't put him off further Arctic travel.

The adversity and deprivation he suffered for his

Arctic ambitions were all too obvious. Like many explorers throughout history, he was away from his family a great deal, and once had a letter from his daughter begging him not to go on any more expeditions. *"I have been looking at your pictures and it seems ten years and I am sick of looking at them,"* she wrote. *"I want to see my father. I don't want people to think me an orphan."*

Peary's wife, a formidable woman named Josephine, remained one of his greatest champions throughout his life. She supported him tirelessly, and raised funds for his expeditions. But, like many explorer's wives, she suffered greatly for her husband's ambitions. During one of Peary's lengthy absences, she gave birth to a daughter. Peary never saw the child, for she died aged only seven months. As well as bearing this tragedy alone, Josephine suffered the strain of not knowing, from one month to the next, whether her husband was still alive. In the days before radio, this was a normal part of the life of any explorer's next of kin. And, in addition to this awful uncertainty, she also had to endure the torment of knowing Peary had an Eskimo mistress, with whom he had had two sons.

The journey that Peary claimed took him to the Pole began in 1908. He had been to the Arctic six times before. His last trip, in 1906, had taken him to latitude 87° 06', less than 3° from the Pole. Peary had learned a lot from these journeys. He designed his own sleds, stoves and clothing, all based closely on tried and trusted designs. He made a habit of sleeping in the open, as many Inuit did. Shunning tents, he only built an igloo when the temperature dropped to extreme levels of cold. He even ate some of his food cold, gnawing on frozen "pemmican" – dried meat and fat pounded into a paste. After all, eating uncooked food saved on fuel.

Ever practical, he chose the members of his team not only for their character, but also for their size. He preferred small, wiry men. They needed less food than big, tall men, and took up less space in an igloo. His ship, the *Roosevelt*, was built on much the same principals. It was short, to make it easier to steer, and its heavy greenwood flanks were strong enough to survive the crushing Arctic ice – the sides were an impressive 76cm (30 inches) thick. It was the only vessel in North America built especially for the northernmost reaches of the Arctic Ocean.

When he set off, aged 52, Peary had already spent much of his life exploring the region. His age was against him, his health was shaky, and his backers were impatient for a success after so many previous failures. He must have known this was going to be his last chance. After a grand send-off from New York, on July 6, 1908, the *Roosevelt* headed for Cape Sheridan on Ellesmere Island's northern coast. Supplies were unloaded and the expedition made their winter headquarters at Cape Colombia. Before the winter came, sled parties were sent off to lay down supplies on the route north.

Then, on February 28, 1909, 24 men set out, with 19 sleds and 133 dogs. Each sled carried 230kg (500lb) of supplies. Peary's plan was for them all to head north, and then return sled by sled, as their food and fuel supplies were used up.

Right from the off, the going across the ice was exceptionally good. It was very cold that season, and the ice had frozen hard – ideal conditions for sleds pulled by dogs. The only problems they encountered were when huge "leads" (cracks in the ice which left gaps of water) opened up in the trail before them. Sometimes they had to wait several days for a lead to close before they could continue going north.

For Peary, everything went brilliantly well. But, for others on his party, the story was not so rosy. One of his colleagues, an American named Ross Marvin, was returning to their base camp, as part of the planned reduction in the number of accompanying sleds. During the journey, Marvin was said to have fallen into a hole in the ice and drowned. The truth, when it came out, was much messier. Accompanied by two Inuit, Marvin had driven his companions on relentlessly. One of the Inuit had repeatedly asked him for permission to rest on the sled, but Marvin had kept refusing. Finally, this man had killed the American and, helped by his companion, he had then dumped the body under the ice.

As Peary's men neared their destination, fewer

and fewer sleds remained. Within 246km (154 miles) of the Pole, Peary sent the *Roosevelt's* Captain, Bob Bartlett, back south. Bartlett had been brought on this trip with an explicit promise that he would be taken to the Pole if circumstances permitted. He was furious to be asked to return south, and never forgave Peary for this decision. (A decade or so later, Bartlet was interviewed about the trip in a restaurant and, when he spoke about Peary, his language became so heated that the head waiter had to ask him to leave.)

Finally, all that remained of the original party was Peary, Henson his servant, who was also a capable translator, four Inuit, five sleds and 40 dogs. Peary claimed to have reached the Pole on April 6, 1909, at around one o'clock in the afternoon, and stayed there some 30 hours.

It was an historic occasion, remembered with a typical lack of modesty by Peary, who summed it up like this: "The discovery of the North Pole stands for the inevitable victory of courage, persistence, endurance, over all obstacles... The discovery of [this]... splendid, frozen jewel of the north, for which through centuries men of every nation have struggled, and suffered and died, is won at last, and is won forever, by the Stars and Stripes!"

It was undoubtedly a significant moment: "The closing of the book on 400 years of history," according to Peary, further blowing his own trumpet.

Peary and his companions raced back to Cape

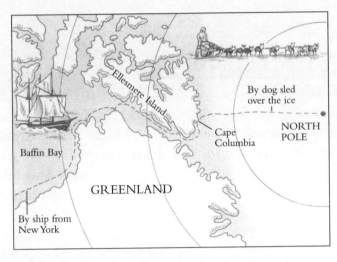

This map shows Peary's claimed route to the North Pole.

Columbia. The journey to the Pole had taken them 40 days. The return took a mere 16. The *Roosevelt* sailed for home, navigating through a sea of fractured ice. By September 6, they had reached Indian Harbor, Labrador, on the very furthest reaches of the international cable network. Here, Peary sent four messages – to his wife Josephine, to *The New York Times*, to the Associated Press news agency, and to the Peary Arctic Club, the organization he had set up to fund his polar ambitions.

But, here at Indian Harbor, Peary also discovered something that was to sour his sense of triumph. Four days earlier, his rival Frederick Cook had announced to the world that he had been to the Pole too – and that he had got there a whole year earlier.

The infamous Dr. Cook

Peary's rival was a likeable doctor of medicine named Frederick Cook, who worked in Brooklyn. The two men knew each other well, and had sailed for the Arctic together over 1891-1892. Quietly ambitious for polar fame himself, Cook had sensed a clear rivalry. For this reason he first turned his attention to the Antarctic. But when circumstances changed it was inevitable that the two would become adversaries. Lacking Peary's prestigious and wealthy backers, Cook set out to raise funds for a polar trek by bringing an Inuit couple to the United States and taking them on a lecture tour. This was exactly the same tactic that had been employed by Charles Hall, and it worked. Public interest in the polar regions was high – they were, after all, among the last places on earth still to be visited by human beings. Audiences flocked to see Cook and his Inuit, and were fascinated by the ingenious construction of Inuit sleds, fur and animal-skin clothing, and kayaks made entirely of seal bone and skin.

Cook's next money-making venture had a tragi-comic edge to it. He hired a 1,100-ton steamer named the *Miranda*, and offered places on a summer cruise to the Arctic for $500 a berth. The *Miranda* set out on July 7, 1894, with 50 passengers, most of them academics or big-game hunters. Several collisions followed, the crew mutinied and went on a drunken rampage after breaking into the wine store, and the *Miranda* struck an iceberg while en route to Greenland. She sank shortly after her passengers had been transferred to a fishing schooner. Amazingly, rather than suing Cook for the shirt off his back, the passengers seemed to revel in their misadventure. Aboard the boat chartered to bring them home, they formed "The Arctic Club", soon to become one of New York's most prestigious societies for explorers. (Honorary members included Shackleton, Scott and Amundsen, all coming up in the next three chapters of this book.)

But before Cook set out on his own expedition, he got the chance to join another one. In 1897, the Belgian government sent the sailing ship *Belgica* to explore Antarctica with an international crew. Cook was taken on board as the ship's surgeon. Few polar vessels had ever ventured this far south. The *Belgica* became trapped in the pack ice and was stranded for the entire Antarctic winter. Men went insane in the endless dark and relentless cold. Cook, however, excelled himself. By all accounts, he was a much valued and useful member of this very difficult expedition. The Norwegian polar explorer Roald Amundsen was among the crew, and wrote of Cook: "*[He was] a man of unfaltering courage, unfailing hope, endless cheerfulness, and unwearied kindness.*" Amundsen even went so far as to attribute the survival of the Belgica's crew to Cook's "*skill, energy and persistence*".

Such reports did much for Cook's burgeoning reputation as an explorer. Further fame followed in 1903, when Cook announced he had climbed Mount McKinley, the highest peak in North America. He wrote a best selling book about it, *To the Top of the Continent*, and was elected president of the American Explorer's Club. Unlike the imperious Peary, whose haughty character was all too obvious, Cook appeared to be a genial, good-natured man. Photographs invariably show him with a smile and a twinkle in his eye, as if he is about to make an amiable quip.

But all this was to change. Such was the "leprous blanket of infamy" that would be heaped on Cook in the years to come, he once, rather pitifully, described himself as "the most shamefully abused man in the history of exploration". Maybe he was, but there was something in his character which led him astray, and which would eventually destroy his reputation as a great explorer.

The first steps to Cook's downfall began in 1907, when he set off from New York to try to reach the North Pole. This change of polar destination was prompted by a meeting with John R. Bradley, a wealthy American gambling-club owner and big-game hunter, who had offered to finance the trip. Bradley suggested they keep the voyage secret so that, if Cook should fail, they could pass off the trip as a hunting expedition. Cook sailed to the Arctic Circle aboard a ship named the *John R. Bradley*, after his backer. Bradley came along too, intending to add some seals, walruses and polar bears to his collection of stuffed animals. By a strange coincidence, the captain of their ship was one Moses Bartlett, cousin of the *Roosevelt's* captain, Bob Bartlett.

Bradley couldn't help boasting about his voyage, and news of Cook's attempt on the Pole reached Peary while his ship, the *Roosevelt*, was holed up in dry dock, undergoing repairs on damage sustained during his last polar attempt. Peary, frustrated by his inability to prevent Cook's voyage, and fearful that he would be beaten to the Pole, huffed and puffed that such a move was "one of which no man with a high or even average sense of honor would be guilty…" Peary had put so much effort into trying to reach the Pole, he felt he was entitled to do so without anyone else trying to get there before him.

Cook, and the ship's cook Rudolph Francke, were dropped off by the *John R. Bradley* in the Inuit village of Anoatok, near Etah, Greenland. After spending the winter there, the two of them, together with nine Inuit, set off for the Pole. At first they went west, via Cape Sabine, then crossed Ellesmere Island, and reached Cape Thomas Hubbard at the tip of Axel Heiberg Island. Here, they left a large supply dump. On March 18, they headed north across the frozen Arctic Ocean on a 1,600km (1,000 mile) round trip to the North Pole. For this daring leap into the unknown, Cook took only two other people. Francke, stricken with scurvy, had given up, as had seven of the Inuit. Accompanying the two sleds and 26 dogs were the Inuit Ahwelah and Etukishook. According to Cook's account, they covered the 800km (500 miles) to the top of the world in 34 days, and claimed to have reached the Pole on April 21, 1908, almost a whole year before Peary.

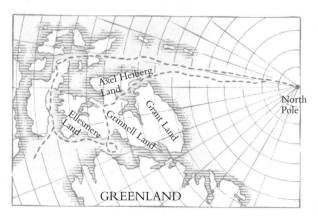

This map shows Cook's claimed route to the Pole. It is based on a drawing by Cook himself. Nowadays, Ellesmere Land, Grinnell Land and Grant Land are known as Ellesmere Island.

The return journey was harrowing. The sleds held only two months' supply of food, but Cook's small party was gone for 14 months. They shot what food they could find, mainly polar bears and seals. But, at several points on the journey, they were so starved that they resorted to eating their candles, and even the leather straps of their sleds.

Cook's party eventually arrived back at the fringes of human habitation in Greenland. From here, he took a boat to Scandinavia via the Shetland Islands, where he sent a telegram announcing his triumph to the world on September 2, 1909. Then he headed for the Danish capital, Copenhagen, where he was greeted by a phalanx of journalists. The Danes hailed him as a great hero, and awards were heaped upon him – he was presented with a gold medal from the Danish Royal Geographical Society, and an honorary degree by the University of Copenhagen. But Cook was not allowed to enjoy his fame for long.

During a banquet to celebrate his triumph, a telegraph arrived with news of Peary's own claim to have been the first to the Pole. This had been announced on September 6, only four days after Cook's own message to the world. An extraordinary photograph was taken mere moments after the telegraph was read out at the banquet. The diners, all dressed in stiff, white shirts and formal dinner jackets, look stunned. Some stare accusingly at Cook. One man is puffing out his cheeks in astonishment. Cook stands in the middle, a garland of flowers draped incongruously around his dinner jacket. He wears an almost comical expression of disappointment and surprise, rather like a pantomime villain about to say, "Curses! Foiled again!"

With hindsight, the battle for credibility was heavily weighted towards Peary right from the start. He was funded by the American Museum of Natural

History, and some of the richest and most respected men in America. He had the blessing of the illustrious National Geographic Society, and had even lunched with President Roosevelt (after whom he had named his ship) on his way out to the Pole. The prestigious *New York Times*, with whom he had a contract to tell his story, also supported him unquestioningly.

Cook, on the other hand, was backed by a raffish big-game hunter who had made his fortune from gambling, which was considered even more disreputable then than it is now. He had returned with no written account of his journey at all, claiming he had left his navigation records and journal in the Arctic. Furthermore, as the controversy raged around him, his two Inuit companions, Ahwelah and Etukishook, later confessed that, in all their time away with him, they had never been out of sight of land. They also claimed that a photograph supposedly showing them at the Pole had been taken with them all perched on top of an igloo, two days' march from land. Then, as a further blow to his reputation, it was revealed that his earlier claim that he had climbed Mount McKinley was a fraud. Photos produced to prove he had reached the summit had been cropped from ones taken on a much lower peak.

Amazingly, all was not lost. Cook was backed by the *New York Times's* major rival, the *New York Herald*.

He stuck to his story about his records, claiming he would have them returned to America as soon as possible. He dismissed Ahwelah and Etukishook's allegations by playing on racist perceptions common among Americans and Europeans at the time. His ignorant Inuit companions had been frightened of straying away from land, explained Cook. To soothe their fears, he had frequently pointed to low-lying clouds on the horizon, telling them that this was land. This was quite plausible – it was not uncommon for seafarers to mistake banks of low clouds for distant land, which would, of course, vanish when they pointed their boats towards them.

The New York Times and *Herald* slugged it out on behalf of their respective champions. The whole western world was riveted by this unseemly and rather comical dispute. The British satirical magazine *Punch*, for example, printed a cartoon showing the Cook and Peary waxworks at Madame Tussaud's punching each other, while British explorer Ernest Shackleton looks on in amazement. To begin with, public opinion was behind Cook. Despite his extremely flimsy evidence, opinion polls at the time generally indicated that eight out of ten people thought Cook had been first to the Pole. The main reason for his success was Peary's unpopularity. Peary's haughty attacks on Cook always lost him support, rather than gaining it. In terms of public appeal, the amiable Cook won hands down against the imperious Peary.

But, over the next few months, Cook's case crumbled – especially when his records failed to appear. His awards were ignominiously withdrawn. Sensing total defeat, he vanished, being reported variously in London, Santiago and his home ground of Brooklyn.

Peary had won. The National Geographic Society pronounced him the first man to the Pole. The United States government awarded him the rank of rear admiral, and he retired with a handsome pension. But his fame and acclaim never bought him any great happiness. His own records, exposed to a glaringly bright light during the controversy with Cook, offered far from conclusive proof that he had actually reached the Pole himself. Recognition came with a slight sense of doubt. Britain's Royal Geographical Society, for example, while hailing him as a great explorer, always hedged their bets when it came to recognizing him as the first man to reach the Pole. Anaemia, first diagnosed by none other than Frederick Cook after an earlier expedition, came back to claim him. Peary died on February 20, 1920. He was 64.

Cook's fate was altogether more tragic. Seeking to make a living in the world of property and land speculation, Cook had sold land to one customer with the assurance that it contained oil. When no oil was found, Cook was charged with fraud, placed on trial in 1923, and found guilty.

The judge at the trial was merciless. "This is one of those times when your peculiar and persuasive personality fails you, doesn't it?" he taunted. "Oh God, Cook, haven't you any sense of decency at all?"

The sentence was harsh: Cook was fined $14,000, and sent to Leavenworth Penitentiary for 14 years and 9 months.

Cook's disgrace was complete. His old friend, the esteemed polar explorer Roald Amundsen, loyally paid him a visit at Leavenworth, while visiting America on a lecture tour. The National Geographical Society immediately cancelled a speaking engagement they had made with him in disgust.

But Cook did not stay in Leavenworth forever. He was still a winning character, and he managed the formidable task of being popular with both the guards and the inmates. He was paroled in 1930, and then given a presidential pardon in 1940. It turned out the land he had sold did contain oil after all – millions of gallons, in fact.

Cook died soon after his presidential pardon, leaving a final taped message to the world: "I have been humiliated and seriously hurt. But that doesn't matter any more. I'm getting old, and what does matter to me is that I want you to believe that I told the truth. I state emphatically that I, Frederick A. Cook, discovered the North Pole."

Nearly a century later, the argument is still to be won conclusively, and modern polar historians have come to ask whether either of them reached the Pole. Cook's own case was pretty much destroyed in the year after he presented it. But Peary's extraordinary speed across the ice on his return journey also seems too good to be true. He kept careless navigational records, with no measurement of longitude, and made no allowances either for the constant drifting of the ice he crossed, or for compass variations caused by the earth's fluctuating magnetic field, for which adjustments are usually made at these latitudes. His lack of "reliable" witnesses (*i.e.* white men who would be able to verify his own sightings) also undermined his case in the eyes of his contemporaries.

When all is said and done – and millions of words have been written on what one writer called "the dispute of the century" – it's unlikely either of them reached the Pole. But Peary probably got considerably closer than Cook.

Amundsen's hollow victory

American sports coach "Red" Saunders once said: "Winning isn't everything. It's the only thing." Saunders had obviously never heard of Roald Amundsen. This tremendously capable Norwegian explorer became the first man to lead a team to the South Pole, beating a rival British team, led by Robert Falcon Scott, by a month or more. Confounding the expectations, and sometimes open scorn, of fellow explorers, Amundsen showed that careful planning and good sense could take five men to the most remote spot on earth with relative ease. Scott's expedition, by contrast, ended in tragedy, his poor planning and misjudgment leading to his own death, and that of four other men with him. Yet although Amundsen won the race to the Pole and brought his team home alive, it was Scott who would be celebrated as a hero − a twist of fate that would have puzzled Saunders.

As a boy, Amundsen had read about the exploits of Sir John Franklin, and was determined to follow in his footsteps. His great hero was fellow Norwegian Fridtjof Nansen, the world-famous Arctic pioneer. Amundsen made his first polar trip in 1898. Aged 25, he had been aboard the *Belgica*, on the Belgian-led international expedition to Antarctica, which had also included Dr. Frederick Cook. The expedition ship was trapped in the pack ice and forced to wait out the long polar winter. And, while some men went insane in the endless dark, and the crew fell to squabbling and scurvy, Amundsen thrived on the hardship. One officer recalled he "was the biggest, the strongest, the bravest, and generally the best-dressed man for sudden emergencies".

Amundsen's lifelong ambition had been to be the first man to reach the North Pole. To this end, in 1910, he had borrowed the Norwegian vessel, the *Fram*, which had been used by Nansen on his intrepid voyage. Amundsen hired a crew, and was all set to sail north when word reached him that Cook and Peary were both claiming they had reached the Arctic Pole. Others would have been crushed by disappointment, but within minutes of hearing the news Amundsen just changed his destination. He would sail south for the Antarctic instead.

In his quest for fame, Amundsen was canny enough to know he had to be sly. The funds to finance his expedition (from both the Norwegian government and private backers) had been for an Arctic trip. Perhaps his backers would withdraw if they knew they were paying for an Antarctic expedition? The British had also made it plain to other nations that they wished to be the first to reach the South Pole. At the time, Britain had an empire which covered a quarter of the world, and the Norwegian government had no wish to upset such a powerful country. But, in particular, Amundsen knew that the British explorer Robert Falcon Scott was preparing for an assault on the South Pole at that very moment. Anything that delayed Amundsen would rob him of the chance of beating Scott to the Pole.

So Amundsen told no one of his change of plan, not even his crew. But some of them must have been puzzled when components for a base hut were brought on board, as were teams of dogs – huts were only put up on land, and there was no land at the North Pole, only frozen sea. And, for Arctic expeditions, dogs were usually acquired nearer the destination.

The *Fram* slipped away from Norway on August 9, 1910, with a crew of 19 men. Only when they reached Madeira, off the coast of Morocco, were the men told of their true destination. Here, Amundsen also notified the Norwegian government, figuring that revealing his plans when he was already well into his journey would prevent them from stopping him continuing on his way.

Amundsen's knowledge of polar travel had led him to believe the best way to travel was with skis and sleds pulled by dogs. This method, perfected by the Arctic inhabitants, seemed so transparently better than any other that he couldn't understand why everyone didn't use it. It was known his rival, Scott, intended to use Manchurian ponies as well as dogs, and to have his men haul sleds to the Pole. (This is known as manhauling.) But one thing about Scott's party did bother Amundsen. The British were also taking three motorized sleds. If these were a success – and so far they were an unknown factor – then there was every chance Scott would reach the Pole before the Norwegians.

The *Fram* sailed to Antarctica through the Ross Sea, taking only a single week to negotiate the pack ice. The crew unloaded their equipment and hut in the Bay of Whales, and named their camp Framheim (meaning "*Fram*'s home"). Then immediately they set about preparing for the trek south and making themselves comfortable for the coming winter. The plan was to lay down supply dumps at intervals along the route, and then wait until the Antarctic spring in September or October, when they would dash for the Pole.

Probably because they came from a country well-used to snow and cold and long, dark nights, the Norwegians adapted very easily to Polar conditions. They worked through blizzards, laying down three hefty supply dumps on the way south to the Pole. When the winter weather forced a stop to the preparation of the route, they retired to the hut. It was uncomfortably crowded, so they built a warren of underground corridors and chambers next to it, hewn from the snow and ice that soon built up around them. Here, there were workshops, a place to cook, a room for the cook's slops, a lavatory, and even a stove-powered sauna. In their underground warren they prepared for the trip, shaving the wood on their sleds to remove any unnecessary weight, until all the sleds were one third lighter.

Amundsen's men passed the winter amiably enough, although they couldn't help noticing that Hjalmar Johansen was keeping an icy distance. Johansen was a friend of Nansen's whom Amundsen had taken on the expedition as a concession to his hero. Johansen had a serious lack of respect for his new leader. This erupted into full-scale contempt after Amundsen began an early – and disastrous – dash for the Pole.

Fearing the British would beat them, the Norwegians began their southward trek in early September – the very beginning of the Antarctic spring. Johansen had cautioned against this. The weather proved too harsh, and Amundsen and his men were forced to return, suffering from frostbite and exhaustion. A bitter argument blew up between Amundsen and Johansen. They quarrelled so fiercely that Amundsen removed Johansen from his South Pole team, and instead sent him and two other members of the expedition to explore an unknown coast to the east.

The source of friction removed, Amundsen's men waited patiently for the season to turn. By October

20, conditions were judged to be right, and the Norwegians set off for the Pole. Along with Amundsen were Olav Bjaarland, Helmer Hanssen, Sverre Hassel and Oskar Wisting, and 52 dogs pulling four sleds. Their supplies had been meticulously packed in the sleds over the winter. The men did not ride the sleds, as this would have created unnecessary additional weight for the dogs to pull. Instead, they ran or skied alongside them. Every sled was pulled by a team of dogs in a fan formation, each dog having its own leash and harness, so that if it fell into a crevasse it wouldn't drag any of its fellows with it.

Amundsen planned a daily rate of 24km (15 miles). He could have gone faster, but didn't want to exhaust the dogs. Right from this second start, luck was with them. They made very good progress and, by November 4, they had reached the last of the dumps laid down the previous autumn. It was 82° south. From here, they managed to advance a further 1° every four days: a distance of roughly 112 km (69 miles). Amundsen decided to set up a new dump at every 1° on the way to the Pole. This way, they would have less to carry with them on their return journey. These dumps were clearly marked by a flag on a stick, and by a series of smaller penants, placed either side of the dump. These markers would direct them back to the dump if their navigation was faulty, or if they became lost in a blizzard.

Each night, when they stopped to make camp, the men would set up their tents and sleep comfortably in sleeping bags made of three layers of fur. At the top of the Axel Heiberg Glacier, half the dogs were shot. With supplies left behind in a trail of dumps, they were simply not needed to pull the sleds anymore. Their bodies were fed to both the other dogs (who had no problem at all about eating their own kind) and the explorers. There were now 18 dogs left, to pull three sleds in teams of six a piece.

But it wasn't all plain sailing. As they neared the Pole, the sleds had to cross a terrifying stretch of ice the men named the Devil's Glacier. Here, crevasses stretched in every direction, often hidden by snow, and all promising a swift demise to anyone unwary enough to plunge into their hidden depths. Hassel and Amundsen, roped together, probed gingerly forward, painstakingly charting a safe route through. Immediately after this obstacle there was a vast plain of thin ice, which the men named the Devil's Ballroom. Here, the surface was often too weak to support the weight of a man, and it was all too easy to plunge down through the ice into a deep crack.

Taking regular sightings with a sextant, they edged towards their goal. Finally, at three o'clock in the afternoon, on December 14, 1911, Amundsen came forward to be the first to stand on a spot they took to be the very bottom of the world. The Norwegians set up a tent over this spot, which they also marked with their national flag. Inside the tent, Amundsen left a letter for the Norwegian monarch, King Haakon VII.

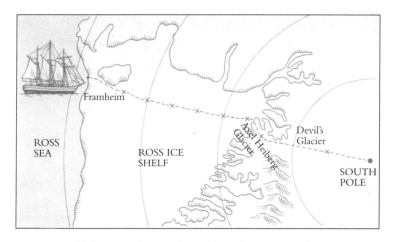

This map shows Amundsen's route to the
South Pole (the crosses mark depots).

With it was a note for Scott, asking him to deliver it.
Ever practical, Amundsen feared his party might not
survive their return journey, and he wanted the
world to know he had made it to the Pole first.

The men set up camp, and celebrated their victory
with a feast of seal meat, and tobacco saved especially
for the occasion. Then, after spending two days taking
readings to ensure they were exactly where they
thought they were, the party set off for home. The
weather on the way back was not as good as it had
been on the way out, but they still made good
progress.

Back at the Framheim base, the men waiting for
them had hardly even begun to wonder when they
might be returning. Quite unexpectedly, they were
roused by a knock on the window. It was four

o'clock in the morning of January 26, 1912. Amundsen and his team had made 2,993km (1,860 miles) in 99 days. Coffee was swiftly brewed. Strangely enough, it was a full hour before anyone got around to asking whether Amundsen had made it to the Pole.

The *Fram* sailed soon after, arriving at Hobart, Tasmania, on March 7. Here, news of Amundsen's success was telegraphed across the world. But Norway's polar heroes were soon to have their extraordinary achievement eclipsed by a glorious failure.

The noble art of dying like a gentleman

From the earliest days of Antarctic exploration, the British behaved as if it was their right to reach the South Pole first. After all, so much of the world was theirs anyway. The president of the Royal Geographical Society, Sir Clements Markham, appointed a Royal Navy officer named Robert Falcon Scott to lead a team to claim the Pole.

Scott, fated to become one of the most famous polar explorers ever, was a complex and not entirely likeable man. Aloof, given to black moods, and steeped in the social snobbery of his era, he was driven by a strong sense of duty and patriotism. A whiff of his haughty character can be gained from this diary entry, where he is describing his expedition deputy Teddy Evans: *"a thoroughly well-meaning little man but rather a duffer in anything but his own peculiar work."* Scott was something of an enigma, though. Despite his starchy character, he married a free-spirited sculptress named Kathleen Bruce.

Scott had first been to Antarctica in 1901. He had set out to explore the interior, but scurvy had undermined his expedition. With him on that trip was Ernest Shackleton (see page 33). Both strong characters, the two men had fallen out, and thereafter became rivals. Another passenger was a young doctor named Edward Wilson, who was a keen ornithologist and a talented artist. Wilson had recently suffered from a bout of tuberculosis, but this didn't stop him from wanting to explore the most hostile region on earth. He and Scott forged a friendship that would endure until their deaths.

Heavily influenced by his mentor, Sir Clements, Scott had a romantic vision of polar exploration, which involved heroically determined men hauling heavy sleds through ice and snow, and triumphing against daunting odds. This approach was exhausting, but other, more practical alternatives were not fully taken up, for reasons which we would now consider questionable. Scott was a product of his age, and carried the usual prejudices of a man of his class and background. Skis, for example, were looked down on as a foreign invention. They were used, for sure, but few of the British party ever really mastered them. Arctic inhabitants had used dogs to pull their sleds. Other polar explorers, such as Peary and Amundsen, had copied this idea with great success. But the British were well-known as a nation of animal lovers. Men like Scott saw dogs as loyal and much-loved companions of the hearth or hunting field. The thought of using them as beasts of burden, driving them to exhaustion and then killing them for food when they were no longer needed, was immensely distasteful to him. This did not stop Scott from using dogs altogether, but he never employed them with the same ruthlessness as his rivals.

By 1910, the South Pole had still to be reached. This was not for want of trying. Scott and Shackleton had both led expeditions, in 1901 and 1907 respectively. The Germans, Swedes and French had also explored the continent. Scott began to plan and recruit for his trip as the decade drew to a close. A meeting with the great Fridjof Nansen convinced him to review some of his prejudices: they would take skis with them after all, and they would also use animals. The sleds would be towed by Manchurian ponies, and they would also take a small team of dogs. Scott still preferred ponies over dogs, despite the fact that Shackleton had used ponies on his 1907 expedition and found them unsuited to polar conditions.

Over 8,000 men volunteered to go on the expedition – most of them from the Royal Navy. By the summer of 1910, Scott had funds, a ship named the *Terra Nova*, and a crew of 67. Among them were his friend, Dr. Wilson, and another veteran from the 1901 expedition, Edgar "Taff" Evans. Scott greatly admired this energetic Welshman, whose resourcefulness and good nature made him an ideal companion. Also among the crew were two men who had made their careers in the British colony of India. No doubt both felt the Antarctic would make a refreshing change from the sultry heat of Asia.

Captain Lawrence "Titus" Oates was a cavalry officer, whose job was to look after the expedition ponies. He seemed to have little idea of what he was letting himself in for, and described the Antarctic climate in a letter to his mother as "*healthy but inclined to be cold*". Lieutenant Henry "Birdy" Bowers was an officer in the Royal Indian Marine. He too had never been to the Antarctic, but he had read a great deal about it.

The *Terra Nova* sailed from Cardiff on June 15, 1910. The Welsh capital was their last port in Britain, as Welsh coal merchants had offered to provide free fuel for the trip. Alongside the 67 crew were 19 ponies, 33 dogs and three motor sleds. Scott hoped that these expensive vehicles, which were then at the cutting edge of transportation technology, would make the business of setting up camps on the way to the Pole much easier. Heavily loaded with provisions for Scott's large crew, the *Terra Nova* took an age to reach its destination. During the voyage, Scott worried constantly about the welfare of his ponies, writing sentimentally about their "*sad, patient eyes*", as they endured the long voyage in cramped stables.

The ship reached Melbourne, Australia, on October 13. Here, Scott discovered that Amundsen was also on the way to the Pole. From this moment on, Scott knew he was in a race. When Dr. Wilson learned of Amundsen's parallel attempt, he wrote in his diary: "*he will probably reach the Pole this year, earlier than we can, for not only will he travel much faster with dogs and expert ski runners than we shall with ponies, but he will be able to start earlier than we can, as we don't want to expose the ponies to any October temperatures."*

They sailed for Antarctica via New Zealand, where Taff Evans disgraced himself. Despite all his great qualities, Evans liked a drink – especially when his ship was in port. On their final stopover before the Pole, he got so drunk that he fell off the ship. Much to the relief of many of Scott's officers, who viewed such failings with distaste, Evans was fired. But he managed to talk Scott into letting him back on board, little suspecting what fate had in store for him.

It took the *Terra Nova* three weeks to make it through the pack ice. (The *Fram* managed it in a week.) The ship reached McMurdo Sound on January 2, 1911, and unloaded its cargo at Cape Evans. Almost at once, disaster struck. No sooner had one of the three motor sleds been taken off the ship than it broke though the ice and sank like a stone.

While Scott prepared for his attempt on the Pole, Amundsen was doing the same over in the Bay of Whales, 650km (400 miles) to the east. Both his and Scott's parties laid down food and fuel depots in a line heading south away from their base camps.

As the polar summer turned to autumn, Scott's team discovered that their ponies had not been a wise choice. On one exploratory trip south, seven out of eight ponies died. The ponies also needed a great deal of looking after, and had to eat hay rather than meat, unlike dogs, who would even eat each other if necessary. The dogs Scott had brought were much faster, and adapted to the freezing conditions with much greater ease. But Scott and his men were never able to train their dogs, nor master their skis, as well as their Norwegian rivals.

The winter brought an end to the laying of depots. Scott's schedule here was not entirely successful. He had intended to set down fuel and food at latitude 80°, in a spot they called One Ton Depot. But the ponies found it such a struggle that the men had to settle for a spot 50 km (30 miles) further north. As the expedition drew to its tragic end, this distance would prove to be vital. Perhaps the ponies would have done better if the men had remembered to bring special pony snowshoes called *trugers*. As it was, only one set was available, the rest having been left at the camp. By the time the stores had been laid, there were only 11 ponies left alive out of the original 19.

During the winter, the men settled into their wooden hut. It was divided down the middle, in the navy tradition, by a row of packing cases. On one side slept the officers, and on the other, the "other ranks".

The Antarctic winter passed and spring came. On October 24, 1911, Scott began his bid for the Pole. Over in the Bay of Whales, Amundsen had left four days earlier – and he had also chosen a starting point noticeably closer to the Pole.

Scott's team had problems right from the start. The motor sleds, on which Scott had spent so much of his expedition budget, set out first. They were supposed to lay down supplies along the route, but lasted a mere five days. Their engines could not cope with the extreme cold of the Antarctic. Scott himself set off with his main party on November 1. Once again the ponies proved to be a disappointment. They sank into the snow and suffered terribly in the cold. By December 9, all of them had had to be shot. The dogs were a greater success, but Scott, still uncomfortable with the idea of using them, sent them back to his base camp on December 11.

Scott's exploration and mapping of the route was far more thorough than Amundsen's, which made his progress slower. As Amundsen neared the Pole, Scott's team were still manhauling heavy sleds up the Beardmore Glacier. When they reached the top, four men returned to Cape Evans, leaving another eight men to press on, in two teams of four. The plan was that, as they neared the Pole, Scott would choose a team of just four men to make the final journey. This reduction in numbers as they grew nearer their destination was designed to ensure that they had the manpower to take sufficient supplies, but also that these supplies would only be needed by a small party on the return journey.

In 1911, radio technology was still very new, and the idea of carrying a radio set out to the Pole to keep in touch with events was unthinkable – so they could not follow Amundsen's progress. Unknown to them, or anyone else at the time, Amundsen reached the Pole on December 14. While Scott was making his final decision on who would accompany him to the Pole, Amundsen was already on his way back to the Norwegian base camp.

The decision as to who would make up the final team was eagerly awaited by the eight men on the British expedition. Scott announced that his own team would accompany him – Evans, Oates and Wilson – and that one man from the other team, "Birdy" Bowers, so-called because he had a big, beaky nose, would also come. Such were the men's intense ambitions to reach the Pole that one of the men not selected, a tough Irish sailor named Thomas Crean, wept when he was told he had not been chosen.

With hindsight, Scott's decision to take an extra man was one of his greatest mistakes, although he had good reasons. Hauling the sleds was exhausting work, which would be done more easily by five men rather than four. Bowers also had a reputation as a skilled navigator. At the time, food supplies looked plentiful. And there was a good mixture of men in the polar party – navy, army, marines, a civilian doctor and, in Evans, one of the "other ranks".

Where Scott's logic was especially faulty was that everything on the trip had been made for four people. The tents were for four, and the sleds carried rations for four. The supply dumps on the way back had also been made assuming there would be four men in the party returning from the Pole. And there was another, unforeseen, problem. One of Scott's chosen team, Taff Evans, had cut his hand, and the wound was festering rather than healing. Evans chose to conceal this injury from Scott – whether from sheer pluck and determination, or from the fear that such a disability would deprive him of a place in the final party, we shall never know. Oates too, was suffering from a wound he had sustained in the Boer War, although this was common knowledge among his companions.

Amundsen was blessed with great good luck on his polar trek, but not Scott. As his five-man team trudged on to the Pole, the fates began to conspire against them, weaving a cruel trap of misfortune and delusion from which they would never escape.

On January 16, a few miles short of their goal, they spotted a black flag in the snow. It was one of Amundsen's food store markers. This evidence of a human presence so near the Pole could only mean one thing – the Norwegians had arrived before them. They reached the Pole the next day, to be confronted by the Norwegians' silk tent. Hopeful that Amundsen might have calculated its position wrongly, they made a thorough check. With mounting disappointment, it gradually dawned on them all that Amundsen had found the exact spot.

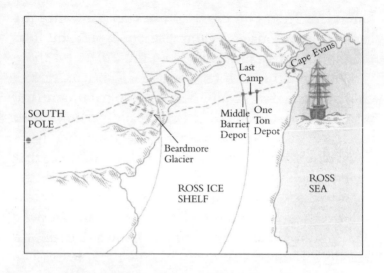

This map shows Scott's route to the South Pole.

The proud Scott was greatly offended by the note from Amundsen asking him to deliver a letter to the Norwegian monarch, King Haakon. It probably didn't occur to Scott that the Norwegians feared for their own return. Then the five men prepared for a ritual team photograph.

These shots taken at the Pole are among the most poignant images from this great era of exploration. Scott and his men pose as if for a school sports photo. Evans and Oates sit cross-legged at the front, with Bowers, Scott and Wilson standing behind them. Scott, ever mindful of his own position, is in the middle of the picture. The men's disappointment is pitifully apparent. Their bodies slump, their hands hang dejectedly at their sides, and they stare into the camera with dour and glum faces, like resentful boys forced out on a rainy picnic.

What photos such as these never convey is the cold. Adding misfortune to their disappointment, the temperature dropped considerably when they arrived. As the men posed for their polar pictures, a sharp, damp wind crept through their clothing and chilled them to the marrow.

Scott's journal of that day conveys some of his disappointment. "*Great God! This is an awful place,*" he wrote, "*and terrible enough for us to have laboured to it without the reward of priority.*" But not only was he distressed at not having got there first, more ominously he also began to worry if they would get back alive. "*I wonder if we can do it,*" he wrote.

Scott was right to worry. He was already suffering from frostbite. The weather was much colder than they had expected. They were one man more than their dwindling food and fuel supplies were intended for. Scurvy was beginning to weaken them. As a final twist, fuel containers they had left at supply depots were now showing a worrying tendency to let fuel evaporate through their frozen leather seals.

Scott's progress had been slow, but this did not stop him from permitting his party to spend half a day collecting rock samples on the Beardmore Glacier on the way back. Time they lost here would prove immensely precious later in the journey. Still, the samples they gathered were of great scientific interest, providing the first clues that Antarctica had once been covered with green forests. Fossilized ferns found among the 16kg (35lbs) of rocks they collected were very similar to ferns found in South Africa, South America, India and Australia, offering proof that Antarctica had once been part of a "supercontinent" made up of all the southern hemisphere land masses.

Much of Antarctica's icy surface is riddled with crevasses. On February 3, Evans and Scott both fell into one. As they were roped to their heavy sled, they did not fall far, and suffered no more than a nasty shock – or so it seemed at the time. Later that day, Evans' actions became particularly odd, or "*rather stupid and incapable*", as Scott recorded sternly in his diary. Given the evidence of his symptoms, it seems Evans's fall left him with serious concussion. Over the next few days, his health deteriorated terribly.

By February 16, Evans was giddy and sick. Pathetically, his ski boots kept falling off his feet, and he was forever lagging behind the rest of the men. This once indefatigable tower of strength had been slowly worn to a frazzle by his festering hand-wound and concussion. It is also likely that Evans, being by far the biggest of the men, most keenly felt the greatly reduced diet now forced upon them. On that February day, as they trudged through the snow, he collapsed. When his companions went back to collect him, they found him kneeling down, his clothing muddled, his speech slurred, and his eyes wild with fear and confusion. As they picked him up to carry him forward, he fell into a coma. He died soon after midnight the next day. The party was back to four.

All of them were now suffering from severe frostbite, but Oates was affected worst of all. His feet were so badly swollen that he had to slit his snow boots to get them on, which did nothing for the boots' ability to keep out the cold and damp. Before the trek had begun, Oates had had a rather macabre conversation with his fellow officers about the responsibility of a man in a sled party who was too weak to keep up with the rest. In the comfort of their winter quarters, Oates had said quite plainly that it was the injured man's duty to kill himself.

Now he was faced with exactly such a situation. He suggested several times that his friends should leave him behind, as he was obviously holding them up. But their own code of loyalty would not let them abandon him. Instead, one morning, after they had made camp at their Middle Barrier Depot, Oates stood up and announced: "I am just going outside and may be some time." No one stopped him as he stumbled into the blizzard outside the tent. Then there were three.

At Middle Barrier Depot, Scott made some alarming calculations. They were 90km (55 miles) from One Ton Depot, where there was enough food and fuel to ensure they would survive their journey. For now, they had supplies for another seven days. In their crippled condition they could cover no more than 10km (six miles) a day. At this rate, at the end of seven days they would have covered 70km (42 miles). They would still be 20km (13 miles) short. The sum added up to almost certain death, as Scott was all too aware. *"I doubt if we can possibly do it,"* he wrote at the time. But, he reasoned, with Oates no longer holding them up, they might still have a chance. Maybe they would have had, if the weather hadn't got worse.

On March 21, two months after the crushing disappointment of finding Amundsen had beaten them to the Pole, Scott and his two remaining companions set up their last camp. They had managed to get to a point 17.5km (11 miles) from One Ton Depot. By now, Scott's frostbite had turned to gangrene. *"Amputation is the least I can hope for,"* he wrote in his diary. And the men's luck, which had so thoroughly deserted them, was not about to turn. There was talk of Bowers, still the strongest of the three, making a go of reaching One Ton Depot to bring back food and fuel. But the blizzard that raged outside their tent blew full and furious for the next ten days. It was the final straw.

To modern eyes, Scott is not a greatly appealing character. He kept a strict distance from men who were beneath him in rank, and he was a disciplinarian whose Royal Navy training led him to insist on unbending routine and etiquette, often to the annoyance and irritation of the men he led. But in his final days, when the prospect of death was utterly certain, his dignified acceptance of his fate was deeply moving. Stuck in their tent, Scott, Bowers and Wilson knew they were going to die as surely as a condemned man knows he is to be executed. But unlike a condemned man, who usually knows when the end is coming, they could only wait for nature to take its course.

Here in the tent, the 43-year-old Scott composed twelve eloquent letters. He wrote to his family, colleagues and friends, and penned comforting words to the wives and mothers of his companions.

To the expedition backers, he wrote: "*we have been to the Pole and we shall die like gentlemen.*"

To his own wife, he wrote: "*I had looked forward to helping you bring [our son] up… Make the boy interested in natural history if you can. It is better than games.*" (She succeeded. Their son, Peter Scott, became a famous wildlife artist and conservationist.) He added, "*You know I cherish no sentimental rubbish about remarriage. When the right man comes to help you in life, you ought to be your happy self again…*" Then he wrote, with painful regret, "*What lots and lots I could tell you of this journey. What tales you would have had for the boy, but oh, what a price to pay.*"

Finally, fully aware of the great interest his demise would spark in the world, he wrote a measured explanation of his actions and their consequences in a final "*Message To The Public*". It concluded, "*Had we lived, I should have had a tale to tell of the hardihood,* endurance, and courage of my companions which would have stirred the heart of every Englishman. These rough notes and our dead bodies must tell the tale…"

He finished his journal with the words: "It seems a pity but I do not think I can write more – R. Scott". The handwriting looks calm, almost unhurried, as if he were writing a leisurely postcard.

There is one final entry underneath, another sentence, this one scrawled in a noticeably more agitated hand, with little attention to punctuation or even capital letters: "Last Entry For Gods Sake look after our people".

It is all too easy to imagine Scott lying starving and shivering to death in his sleeping bag, tormented by his gangrenous foot and by his failure, full of remorse for the men who were dying with him and the family he would leave behind. Perhaps, days later, he roused himself, slowly and agonizingly, to add that final message to the world with clumsy, freezing fingers.

Over the weeks that followed, the tent was half-covered by successive snow storms. Its tip was eventually spotted eight months later, on November 12, by a search team from the Terra Nova. Edward Atkinson, the expedition surgeon, was the first to enter. Preserved by the extreme cold, Bowers and Wilson looked as if they were sleeping peacefully. Scott, his face contorted, was twisted half-out of his sleeping bag. His had evidently not been an easy end.

His diary lay beneath his shoulders. Something everyone noted about the interior was how tidy it was. Clearly Scott's regime of ship-shape neatness had been kept up to the end.

The tent had an outer and inner layer. The search team removed the outer layer and took it with them, along with the men's journals, letters, photographic plates and rock samples. The inner layer they let fall over the three dead men, and a cairn of stones, topped by a cross made of skis, was built over the spot. Then the search team journeyed on to Middle Barrier Depot. Of Oates there was no sign, although they did find his sleeping bag.

The expedition was expected back in New Zealand in April 1913. Like the rest of the world, Kathleen Scott was ignorant of her husband's fate, and set out from England in January of that year to meet him. The *Terra Nova* carried no radio, so the crew was only able to pass on the news when they returned to New Zealand. So Kathleen Scott was aboard a ship in the Pacific when a telegraph informing her of Scott's death reached her, on February 19.

In Britain, the news was greeted with widespread disappointment and led to huge public displays of grief. The outer layer of Scott's tent was erected at the Earl's Court Exhibition Centre in London, and thousands filed silently past this canvas shrine. Reports that his expedition was £30,000 in debt led to a massive outpouring of donations, which eventually raised £75,500. Such was the surplus that, after the expenses had been paid, wages settled and funds provided for relatives, there was enough left over to form the Scott Polar Research Institute in Cambridge. There is a small public museum there now, containing, among other items, Oates's sleeping bag.

The tragedy robbed Amundsen of his victory. Eclipsed by the stoic heroism of the beaten Scott, the Norwegian was often ridiculed. When Amundsen was present at a dinner given by Britain's Royal Geographical Society, then the most prestigious scientific and exploratory organization in the world, a toast was proposed, not to Amundsen, but to the dogs who had pulled him to the Pole. The British, in their pride, could not forgive the Norwegians for reaching the Pole first, and with dogs. It seemed to them to be, in a phrase popular at the time, "unsporting".

Amundsen was to die on yet another polar escapade, this time on a flight to the Arctic to rescue the Italian airship designer Umberto Nobile (see pages 100-111) in 1928. The rest of the men with him at the Pole died in obscurity. Scott and his four companions were immortalized, despite their failure, perhaps proving the old saying that: "It's not the winning that counts, but the taking part". In their case, it had proved to be all too true.

"What the ice gets, the ice keeps"

Frank Worsley lay on his hotel bed, sleeping the unsettled slumber of a deep-water sailor away from the sea. He was in London on shore leave. It was the summer of 1914 and, all around, there was talk of war. Worsley, a born adventurer from New Zealand, who had been at sea since he was 16, sensed interesting times ahead.

As he drifted through the night, a strange dream disturbed his restless sleep. He was at the wheel of a sailing ship, but the boat was not at sea. It was slowly edging down Burlington Street, off London's famous Regent Street. All around were huge, glacial ice-blocks, and Worsley needed all his skill as a steersman to avoid them.

He woke the next morning, threw on his clothes, and hurried down to Burlington Street. There, a sign on a door reading "Imperial Trans-Antarctic Expedition" caught his eye. Worsley was immediately drawn inside, and the first person he saw was Sir Ernest Shackleton, an adventurer and polar explorer of some renown. Shackleton had been to the Antarctic twice before, with Robert Falcon Scott in 1901, and as leader of his own expedition over 1907-

1909. With both Poles now "conquered", he was planning one last, epic trip – the crossing of the entire Antarctic continent. It was a venture Shackleton described as "the largest and most striking of all journeys". An explorer by profession, he was sure it would bring him both lasting fame and financial security.

The two men struck up an instant rapport, and Worsley recalled, "The moment I set eyes on him, I knew that he was a man with whom I should be proud to work." Shackleton, who hired his crews on gut instinct, knew at once that Worsley was his sort of fellow. Worsley was taken on as captain of the expedition vessel, the *Endurance*.

Fifteen months later, the two men and their crew were stranded on an ice floe, and the *Endurance* was about to sink through the ice into the freezing waters of the Weddell Sea. They were hundreds of miles from any other humans, totally without hope of rescue in the cruellest environment on earth.

Shackleton turned to Worsley and said wistfully, "Perhaps it's a pity, skipper, that you dreamed a dream that sent you to Burlington Street that morning we met."

Worsley replied, with no hesitation, "No, I've never regretted it, and never shall, even if we don't get through."

Shackleton had that effect on his colleagues – he inspired a deep, fierce loyalty. In the terrible circumstances they now faced, he would need every ounce of his ability and charisma to hold his team together.

The Imperial Trans-Antarctic Expedition had set sail from London in August 1914 – the very month the First World War broke out. On hearing the news, Shackleton immediately offered to make his ship and crew available for the war, but received a one word reply from the British Admiralty: "Proceed". And so the *Endurance* sailed away from England, leaving a sedate, elegant world of blooming prosperity, straw boaters, brass bands and seaside promenades, which the coming war would change forever.

Aboard the ship were 29 men – a hand-picked selection of officers, seamen, scientists and craftsmen, as well as a photographer and artist. The ship's carpenter, an irascible Scot named "Chippy" McNeish, also brought his cat, known to everyone as Mrs. Chippy.

Shackleton's plan was a bold one. There had been much to learn from recent polar successes and failures, and the Imperial Trans-Antarctic Expedition intended to cross the South Pole using a team of nearly 70 sled dogs. These would haul a six-man party over the Pole. The team would set out from the Weddell Sea and head for the Ross Ice Shelf and Ross Sea. Here, another ship, the *Aurora*, would be waiting to ferry them home. As they set out from the west, a team from the *Aurora* was to lay down a series of depots on the route back to the Ross Sea – places for the sled team to replenish their supplies and rest on the way back to safety.

Shackleton fitted his chosen role of adventurer and seafarer perfectly. He exuded great determination and sense of purpose. The Shackleton family motto was "By endurance we conquer", and he did everything to live up to it. Of medium build, but solid, he had a handsome, brooding face, with a square, forceful jaw. A manly character through and through, when first shown his new-born son, Raymond, he remarked that the baby had "good fists for fighting". But formidable and forbidding though he could be, he had a generous nature and a wry wit. When presented with stowaway Pierce Blackboro, who had sneaked aboard the *Endurance* in Buenos Aires, he growled: "If we run out of food and anyone has to be eaten, you'll be the first."

Exploring was his livelihood and passion. "You cannot imagine what it is like to walk in places where no man has walked before," he once confided to his sister. But he also said, "Sometimes I think I'm no good at anything, except being away in the wilds." It was a reckless way of life that would cost him and his family dear.

By the time the *Endurance* reached the Antarctic island of South Georgia, it was November. Here, the ramshackle whaling station at Grytviken, where the bodies of whales were stripped of their oil and blubber, provided a last, superficial glimpse of civilization. The news there was that the Weddell Sea was heavy with ice, and a route through to Antarctica would not be easy. Shackleton hesitated. This was not a good omen. But, if he turned back, he might never have the chance to go again. He had already failed to reach his objective on previous polar expeditions. He was now 40 years old, and his health was not improving. He had staked everything he had on this trip. Driven by the conviction that this would be his last chance for polar glory, he set out from Grytviken on December 5, at the height of the polar summer. If the ice was bad now, it was not going to get any better.

As the *Endurance* sailed south, the crew were treated to a fantastic display of the Antarctic at its most benign and brilliant. As the ship forged a route through the half-frozen sea, they passed huge, gleaming icebergs, cut by the wind and waves into fantastic, towering sculptures. The perpetual daylight of the polar summer often cast a beautiful pink glow over these bergs and ice floes. The sea bubbled and teamed with life. Huge whales, some twice the length of the ship, would pass by, their blow holes spouting fountains of steam. As albatross and petrels circled above, lazy seals basking on the ice floes would raise a sleepy head to watch them pass. When the seals were not to be seen, penguins (the seals' main prey) would slither and waddle across the ice, croaking out to the ship as it passed. Best of all was the strange phenomenon of the ice shower, when moisture in the air would freeze into ice crystals and float slowly down in a sparkling, magical haze.

But, as Christmas approached, it became obvious that the *Endurance* was making very slow progress. On January 18, 1915, only 50km (30 miles) from the coast, ice closed in around the ship. In a single night the temperature dropped by 40°C (72°F). The crew was about to see a very different side of the Antarctic. They attacked the ice that surrounded the ship with picks, shovels and saws. But, after an entire 48 hours of digging and sawing, there was no doubt that the *Endurance* was stuck solid – "like an almond in the middle of a chocolate bar", as one member of the crew put it.

The days were changing, too. Night fell for brief but lengthening periods, and the once plentiful seals and birds that surrounded the ship were now infrequent visitors. Their animal instincts were telling them this frozen world would soon be uninhabitable, and they were heading north to warmer waters. The *Endurance*'s crew could only stay and prepare for whatever the polar winter could throw at them.

They were so close to land that the coast could sometimes even be seen from the ship. In clear water, it would have taken less than a day to reach. But Shackleton never made his frustrations known. His job was to lead his men, and he did this by projecting an apparently effortless optimism. He knew that the coming winter was going to be very difficult, but he had prepared for it well. Ever mindful of the fate of the crew of the *Belgica* (see page 42), he was determined to keep his men in good spirits. There was a generous library on the *Endurance* and, during the day, men were busied with a well-ordered routine keeping the ship in good condition. Football matches and dog sled races were also played out on the ice. The men began to forge close working relationships with their dogs, and many built elaborate ice kennels for them. Puppies were born, much to everyone's delight. In the evening there were gramophone concerts, or the men would all sing along as meteorologist Leonard Hussey played the banjo.

Shackleton had seen how Scott had bred resentment among some of his men with his authoritarian style of leadership. In contrast, Shackleton worked side-by-side with his crew, and left no one in any doubt that their lives, rather than the aims of his expedition, were his most important concern.

On the darkest day of the polar winter, June 22, there was not a fleck of light in the sky. Shackleton declared it a day of celebration. The ship's mess was decorated with flags and bunting. An improvised stage was constructed and many of the crew came forward to do a turn. Appearing dressed up as a penniless vagabond, a Methodist minister, a crazy professor, and a female flamenco dancer, the men drank and sang their way through the polar night.

Officer Lionel Greenstreet recorded in his diary: "*We laughed until the tears ran down our cheeks.*" These, clearly, were men determined not to let their fearful circumstances get them down.

The ship's crew may have been in good spirits, but the *Endurance* itself was ailing badly. The ship had been built of greenheart – an especially tough wood – but even this was not strong enough to withstand the crushing pressure of thousands of tons of pack ice pressing around the hull. This was now building up so much that the ship was being squeezed to destruction. Some polar ships had been built with hulls designed to rise above crushing pack ice. Not so with the *Endurance*. Deck planks or hull timbers would split with sudden, ferocious cracks like gunshots. Once again, the men tried to dig the ice away from the hull to ease the pressure on their ship, but it was an endless and pointless task.

In the midst of an interminable July blizzard, Shackleton confided in Captain Worsley, "The ship can't live like this, skipper. It's only a matter of time. What the ice gets, the ice keeps."

By the end of October, the *Endurance* had ceased to be a safe place to live. It had seen them through the winter, but now the order was given to abandon ship. Supplies, sleds, three of the ship's large lifeboats, the dogs, puppies and ship's cat, all were bundled overboard. Tents were set up on the ice, near to the ship. In another stroke of canny leadership,

Shackleton announced that they would draw lots to divide up the sleeping bags. The *Endurance* carried both wool and fur sleeping bags, but the fur ones were much warmer. The draw was fixed. All the officers got wool sleeping bags – almost all the men got fur.

But there were difficult decisions to be made. In their perilous circumstances, there was little room for sentimentality. Shackleton decided that the puppies and the cat would have to be shot. His decision to kill the animals was a considerable blow to the crew's shaky morale. His men were, in the main, hardened sea dogs, few of whom were married or had children. In the robust, all-male world of the *Endurance*, the puppies and cat had provided an opportunity for the crew to show a softer side. On the journey over, the cat had fallen overboard, and the ship had turned around to rescue her from the Atlantic. This time, Mrs. Chippy was not so lucky.

With the ship creaking and groaning behind him, like a huge, beleaguered animal in its death throes, Shackleton called his men together. With no trace of drama or regret, he told them plainly that the *Endurance* could no longer carry them, so now they, and their dogs and sleds, were going home. Put so plainly, it sounded like a reasonable, logical course of action. But the reality was very different. Hauling the heavy sleds was hot, sweaty, exhausting work. They made such slow progress across the ice fields that, even after three days, they could still see their ship.

Shackleton had a talent for constantly revising his objectives. Heading for safety across the frozen sea with the sleds and dogs was clearly not going to work. They returned to the ship – now a frozen, eerie hulk, its once-cozy interior covered with a veneer of ice – and rescued many of the supplies that had been left behind. Expedition photographer Frank Hurley had left many beautiful photographic plates in the ship. (Known as glass-plate negatives, these heavy, pane-of-glass sized images produced much better photographs than the recently invented photographic film.) When Hurley entered the *Endurance*'s frozen interior, he found the storage area where he'd left the plates under 1.2m (4ft) of mushy ice and water. There was nothing else to do but strip down to his underwear and dive in to get them.

On November 21, the broken, waterlogged hulk finally sank. Surrounded by the wreckage of fallen masts and rigging, the bow went down into the icy water, which could be briefly glimpsed, and the stern rose high in the air. At this point, the heavy, steel bolts which anchored the *Endurance's* powerful steam-engine in place were wrenched out. With a terrifying sound of splintering wood, the iron engine dropped through deck partitions into the now-vertical bow, dragging the ship down to the black bottom of the Weddell Sea. It was a heart-breaking moment. Shackleton wrote in his journal: "*At 5:00pm she went down. I cannot write about it.*" For a brief while there was a small hole in the ice, but it soon closed. The *Endurance* was gone.

The crew settled uneasily into their new home on the ice. The frozen crust was 1.5m (5ft) thick, and might have given the impression they were on solid ground. But seeing the ship go down was a graphic reminder that, below them, there was a vast sea of freezing water. Still, Shackleton made every effort to keep his men cheerful, despite his own failing health. (Soon after the *Endurance* sank, a bout of sciatica forced him to spend two weeks in his tent.)

Another attempt to march north seemed to be the only thing left to do. But the ship's lifeboats each weighed at least a ton. They had to be hauled along by teams of men in harness, which was terribly difficult to do over rough ice. And, as they tried to start their long journey home yet again, Shackleton was faced with open mutiny. Chippy McNeish, still bitter about the death of his cat, refused to haul the boats. He told Shackleton his duty to him was relinquished now that the ship had sunk. Shackleton knew that the only hope they had of getting back alive was to work together as a team. If McNeish was allowed to become the focus for other resentful crew members, the party would split into warring factions, and they would all be doomed. Forceful action was required. McNeish was bluntly told he would be shot if he did not obey orders.

Shackleton then called his men together. He

reassured them that they would still be paid until they reached a safe port, and explained that it was essential for everyone to work together. Finally, he announced that the hauling would stop. It was too exhausting. They would simply have to drift north with the ice, as they had been doing when the *Endurance* was still afloat, and then take to the boats when the pack began to break up.

Shackleton may have seemed forceful and in command but, that night, he was so shaken by McNeish's rebellion that he could not sleep. There were difficult decisions to make, too. With the idea of sledding north abandoned, there was no sense in continuing to feed their teams of dogs. They had enough problems keeping themselves alive on the limited supply of seals and penguins they managed to catch. Shooting the dogs was heart-wrenching, but kinder than letting them loose to starve to death in the ice. Frank Wild, the expedition second-in-command, was the executioner. He wrote in his journal: "*I have known many men I would rather shoot than the worst of the dogs. It was the worst job I have ever had in my life.*"

For four months, the men drifted on the ice. At night, they curled up in their sleeping bags and tried to gain enough warmth to sleep. They ate a monotonous diet of seal meat, supplemented by their dwindling food supplies, and prayed that they would soon reach the open sea. In early April, just as the polar summer was drawing to an end, the ice they stood on began to move with the swell of the ocean. Men began to feel seasick, but this could only mean they were nearing open water. On April 9, the boats were readied and set out to sea. They had been stranded on the ice for 14 months. Now, they were finally free – but free to do what?

The journey that followed was seven days of freezing, wet torment. 240km (150 miles) to the north lay Snow Hill Island. Although the island was uninhabited, they knew supplies had been left there to help any shipwrecked mariners. It was here they set their sights. By day, they pushed on through towering seas, while men not rowing bailed furiously to keep their open boats afloat. By night, they clambered aboard passing ice floes, to shiver in their tents. But one night there was a loud crack, and the ice split through the middle of a tent. Ernest Holness, one of the *Endurance's* stokers, fell through. He floundered in the freezing sea, trapped in his soaking sleeping bag, stunned almost to paralysis by the shock of the icy water. Shackleton ran over, thrust a hand into the gap, and pulled Holness out, bag and all. An instant later, the split closed up with a crash. From then on, the men slept in the boats.

Perhaps it was the thought that they were actually doing something, rather than just passively drifting, that kept the crew going. Their hands were so cold that they had to be chipped off the oars at the end of a shift. Dysentery swept through the boats, and everyone suffered from a raging thirst and hunger. Now, at night, the three boats were roped together to prevent them from drifting apart. But as men tried to sleep they would be disturbed by killer whales, which blew air through their blow holes "like suddenly escaping steam". The whales brushed against the boats, threatening to sever the ropes that held them together. Occasionally they would peer out of the water, presenting the crew with a huge, dark maw and sharp, white, gleaming teeth. Men wept in despair, and the threat of death hung in the air. His boats swamped and his men nearly finished, Shackleton changed his plans again. If they kept on to Snow Hill Island, they would not all reach there alive. Instead, the boats altered course for Elephant Island, which was nearer, but had no supplies.

On their seventh day at sea, the brooding cliffs of Elephant Island loomed before them. This barren slab of rock, ice and snow would have to serve as their new home. The boats forged ashore through swirling reefs and treacherous currents, and the men staggered onto the shingle beach, some delirious with joy. It was the first time any of them had stood on solid land for 497 days. They had had yet another close escape. One of Shackleton's men estimated that some of them would have died within a day if they had not landed on the island.

It had been impossible to cook at sea but, once ashore, hot drinks and food were prepared. Tents were quickly set up, and each man could feel his strength returning. But Elephant Island was not a place where anyone would wish to stay, and the men soon grew to loathe it. Aside from elephant seals (from which the island took its name) and penguins, there was almost nothing there to eat. Constant sleet, snow and rain hammered down. And the rock was not on any known shipping route, so there was still no chance of rescue. So Shackleton did the only thing he could do. He prepared to set out to an inhabited island.

There were several options open to him, all of which were terribly dangerous. The nearest inhabited land was near Cape Horn, on the tip of South America. But the wind blew constantly east on the route to the Cape, making it impossible to reach in a small boat coming from the opposite direction. An alternative destination was the island of South Georgia. It was from here that they had set off for the South Pole, in the faraway days of December, 1914. This, at least, was in the path of the wind – but it was 1,300km (800 miles) away, across one of the most dangerous oceans on earth.

Not all of them would go, of course. Shackleton decided six men would make the journey. Frank Worsley would come, and second officer Thomas Crean, who had been with Scott on his final, fatal expedition. Shackleton also took a couple of men who were known troublemakers, including the quarrelsome carpenter, Chippy McNeish. But, for all his faults, McNeish was proving to be indispensable.

He had a genius for improvisation. Such was his skill and confidence with wood that, while she was stranded, he had offered to build a smaller ship from the remains of the *Endurance*. Now he set to work on the biggest lifeboat, the *James Caird*, to make it as seaworthy as possible for the journey ahead. The gunnels (sides) were raised with wood from packing cases, and bits and pieces from the other two boats were taken to strengthen the hull. Oil paint and seal blood was used to make the new seams watertight.

Leaving the rest of the men behind with the expedition second-in-command, Frank Wild, the *James Caird* put to sea on April 24, 1916. Shackleton and his small crew watched the 21 men left behind wave them off until they were out of sight. Perhaps it was lucky they could not see that many of the men had tears streaming down their faces. Most of those on the shore were convinced they would never see the crew of the *James Caird* again.

The journey was every bit as dreadful as everyone expected. They set out in calm weather, but it soon turned stormy. Huge waves dwarfed the tiny boat, and freezing rain constantly hammered down on them. The six men took turns to row and steer and bail and sleep – four hours on, and four hours off – but there was not a single moment when they were not soaking and freezing. How they did not succumb to hypothermia or frostbite remains a mystery. Most extraordinary of all, navigator Frank Worsley was only able to take four sightings with his sextant in over two weeks at sea. For the rest of the time he steered by "dead reckoning", a sailor's term meaning guesswork and instinct.

On the 14th day of the journey, seaweed floated past the boat – a sure sign that land was near. But, as the cliffs of South Georgia began to peer over the horizon and the men could sense their troubles were nearly over, a ferocious storm blew up. Again, Frank Worsley was the hero of the hour. With extraordinary skill, he managed to steer the *James Caird* away from reefs and rocks that would have dashed the men to death. Elsewhere off South Georgia, the same storm claimed a 500-ton steamer.

On the evening of May 10, after 17 days at sea, they landed at King Haakon Bay on South Georgia. It was the wrong side of the island, 35km (22 miles) from Stromness, the nearest inhabited settlement, but it would have to do. After four days recovering from the trip, Shackleton, Worsley and Crean felt strong enough to set out for help. The boat, and the other men, were no longer in any state to take to sea, so the three of them would have to go on foot.

Between them and rescue lay a series of steep mountain peaks and glaciers – an uncharted island interior no one had ever crossed. But Shackleton was not a man to let such details bother him. After McNeish had fitted screws from the *James Caird* to their boots, to act as crude crampons, Shackleton,

Worsley and Crean set off under a luminous full moon.

The journey they made would not be repeated until 1955, and only then by experienced and fully-equipped mountain climbers. The three men waded through snow, dodging glaciers and precipices, knowing that to stop would be to risk death from exposure. High on a ridge and tiring fast in an icy wind, Shackleton took a huge, devil-may-care risk. Knowing that they would freeze to death if they stayed there much longer, he coiled his rope to make an improvised toboggan. All three sat on it, and shot down a steep snow slope to the valley below. They could have been dashed to pieces on sharp rocks, or fallen into a crevasse or over a cliff. But they didn't. Their luck held.

By daybreak, they were looking down on Fortuna Bay, near to Stromness and rescue. At seven o'clock that morning, they heard the steam whistle that signalled the start of the morning shift at the whaling station. It was their first indication of other human life since December 1914.

At three o'clock on the afternoon of May 20, 1916, three bedraggled, hairy men staggered into Stromness. They were black from the soot of their blubber stoves, stinking abominably, their clothes in tatters. They were such a terrifying sight that children ran screaming away from them. Factory manager

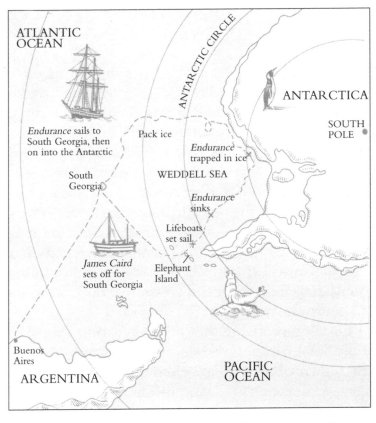

This map shows the progress of Shackleton's expedition
to the Antarctic, starting from Buenos Aires.

Thoralf **Sörlle**, who knew Shackleton well, was
summoned to meet them.

"Who on earth are you?" he demanded, when
confronted with the bizarre strangers.

One came forward and said, plainly, "My name is
Ernest Shackleton."

Sörlle burst into tears. These men had come back from the dead.

The wait at Elephant Island was an unimaginable ordeal. After the first month, each man would awake thinking today was the day they would be rescued. But days, weeks and months went by, and still no one came. By August, Frank Wild had reluctantly come to the conclusion that the *James Caird* had been lost. He began to plan another voyage away from their island prison. The truth, however, was more mundane. It took Shackleton three months and four attempts to get through the storms and ice, and onto Elephant Island. Eventually, he had to travel to Punta Arenas, in Chile, to obtain a boat equipped to make the journey.

On August 30, the men were preparing a meal of boiled seal backbone when a cry went up: "A ship!" Only then could anyone believe they would ever see their homes and families again. Shackleton was there on the rescue ship to greet them, barely able to speak. *"Not a man lost, and we have been through Hell,"* he wrote to his wife soon afterwards. His ambitious journey had failed. No one, in fact, would cross the Antarctic until 1958. But his other ambition – to get every single member of his crew back to safety – had been achieved against extraordinary odds.

At Stromness, Shackleton had asked Sörlle when the war had ended.

"The war is not over,"he had answered, "Millions are being killed. Europe is crazy. The world is crazy."

So the crew of the *Endurance* sailed back to a dreary, war-torn country, which was indifferent to their ordeal. Heroes were dying everyday on the Western Front. Amid the barbed wire, tanks and poison gas of the trenches, adventurers like Shackleton were men out of time.

Flying and floating to the Pole

The first powered flight was made at the very beginning of the 20th century, by the Wright Brothers of Kittihawk, Ohio. Then, the outbreak of the First World War in 1914 transformed the science of aeronautics. Before the war, crude, single-engine, canvas-and-wire flying machines could barely limp across the English Channel. Yet, in 1919, only a year after the war ended, a four-engine British bomber flew across the Atlantic Ocean in an astounding 16 hours. This emerging new technology aroused great interest among polar explorers.

Reaching the Poles by air was not an entirely new idea. A Swede, Salomon Andrée, had attempted to go to the North Pole by balloon many years before. He and two companions, Knut Fraenkel and Nils Strindberg, had set off from the small island of Danskøya, off Spitsbergen, on July 11, 1897. After two years without news, it was assumed the men had perished. Only in 1930 did their fate become known, when their remains, some photographs and their diaries, were found by a Norwegian seal ship. Three days into the flight, when they had covered 830km (520 miles), the balloon crashed. Lacking any means of summoning help, the men walked south. After a gruelling three months, they reached the island of Kvitøya, where they all died.

Twenty years on from Andrée's flight, Roald Amundsen was determined to do better. The distinguished polar explorer had entered into a partnership with Lincoln Ellsworth, a wealthy American. Ellsworth, the son of a Chicago millionaire, was keen to investigate how the North Pole could be reached by air.

Their initial venture ended in near tragedy. They acquired two Dornier-Wal seaplanes to fly to the Pole. En route, the planes landed on the ice, where one of them was damaged beyond repair. The explorers, and their four crew mates, had to make an improvised runway. The remaining plane, now loaded with six people instead of three, took off, clearing the runway and an iceberg in their path by a whisker. When they returned, after 26 days away, they were greeted like men back from the dead. The narrow escape merely whetted their appetite for another attempt. This time, they thought, they would try with an airship.

In the 1920s, airships had become the most exciting prospect in aeronautics. Developed as bombers during the First World War, these flying machines were raised high into the air by bags of lighter-than-air gas, such as hydrogen, and pushed through the sky by propellers. After the war, airships began to make transoceanic flights, and were increasingly thought of as passenger liners in the sky.

At the time, the finest airships in the world were built in Italy. So Amundsen and Ellsworth approached a well-known Italian airship designer named Umberto Nobile. Rather than designing a new ship, Nobile talked them into using one he had already built, which they bought second-hand for $75,000. They also decided to take Nobile along on the flight, reasoning that the designer of the airship would be the best possible person to have around if anything went wrong. The airship was given the Norwegian registration number N-1. Amundsen and Ellsworth thought something more romantic was required for their expedition, so the craft was named *Norge*, meaning Norway.

Nobile was a small, self-important and excitable man, and he attempted to dominate the expedition. This led to much ill feeling between him and Ellsworth and Amundsen, who regarded him as a hired hand. But, as it happened, Nobile had a very useful ally in his quest for personal fame. Benito Mussolini, the fascist dictator of Italy, realized that an Italian at the Pole, in an Italian-designed flying machine, would bring his country much prestige. Nobile's flight with Amundsen and Ellsworth would be a classic opportunity for propaganda. As far as the rest of the world was concerned, the flight was known as the Amundsen-Ellsworth Expedition, but in Italy it was reported as the Amundsen-Ellsworth-

Nobile Expedition.

Amundsen and Ellsworth had another rival in their quest to reach the Pole by air: US Navy pilot Richard Byrd. In May 1926, as they prepared to set off from the Bay of Kings, in Spitsbergen, Byrd arrived with his co-pilot, Floyd Bennet. Byrd and Bennet took off shortly after midnight on May 10, returning just after four o' clock that afternoon. The Pole, they reported, had been reached. News flashed around the world, and the two men were hailed as heroes. Only after Byrd's death in 1957 did the truth about the flight come out. Byrd's records of the flight had been long disputed. Aeronautical scientists had already suspected, at best, faulty readings, at worst, fraud. After Byrd's death, Bennet confessed that his leader had just told him to fly around out of sight of land long enough for the plane to have flown to the Pole and back.

Still, said Amundsen and Ellsworth, if they could not be the first to fly to the Pole, they would be the first to get there in an airship. They took off with Nobile and their crew the very next day, May 12, just after midnight. Their intention was to fly over the Pole and then on to Alaska. By half past one in the morning, the *Norge* was indeed circling the Pole. A landing was not attempted, but the craft flew low and Norwegian, American and Italian national flags on poles, weighted to land upright and stick in the snow, were dropped from the cabin.

The occasion was marred by an unseemly dispute over the size of the flags. Nobile had specifically told Amundsen and Ellsworth that they could only bring small, bath-towel sized flags, as the weight the airship carried had to be kept to a minimum. (He had already forbidden them warm flying clothes for this reason, although he and fellow Italian crew members wore heavy fur outfits.) But, when the time came, Nobile appeared with a heavy wooden case containing a huge Italian flag, the size of a bedsheet, which dwarfed the others.

The journey away from the Pole was fraught. Ice formed on the *Norge*, including on the radio antenna, which prevented transmissions. More alarmingly, chunks of ice were flung from the propellers into the body of the airship. It seemed only a matter of time before one of the hydrogen bags that lifted the craft into the air would be pierced.

But their luck held. The *Norge* reached Alaska on May 14, where the local Inuit were amazed by the airship, which they called a flying whale. The expedition was hailed as a huge success. Amundsen, Ellsworth, Nobile and their crew had covered 4,956km (3,180 miles) in just over 70 hours.

On their return to the USA, Mussolini promoted Nobile to the rank of general, and instructed him to go on a lecture tour of the "Italian colonies" there. This was a typical piece of fascist bluster. What Mussolini meant by "colonies" were those areas of the United States where there were large numbers of

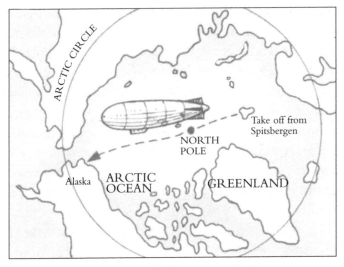

This map shows the flight of the airship *Norge*.

Italian immigrants.

Amundsen and Ellsworth greeted the American press wearing shabby, dirty clothing. Nobile had insisted that, to save weight, they should not bring any spare clothes. Again, he outraged his colleagues by appearing in a full ceremonial uniform that he had sneaked aboard. Because he was so smartly dressed, many people assumed Nobile was in charge of the expedition, and he did everything he could to claim credit for both the planning and leadership of the trip. Nobile might have built the machine that took them to the Pole and back, but Amundsen and Ellsworth must have regretted the day they ever set eyes on him.

The dispute over who was to gain the greatest

credit for the 1926 flight bothered Nobile so much that he was determined to mount his own Italian-only flight to the Pole. Another airship was procured, this one named *Italia*. In mid-May 1928, he made several successful Arctic flights around the Russian Arctic islands, with a mainly Italian crew.

Then, on May 23, Nobile and 16 comrades set off for the Pole, along with Nobile's dog, Titina, who went everywhere with him. Accompanying them as far as it was able was a support ship named the *Città di Milano*. There was little interest in this attempt, even in Italy. After all, it had already been done two years earlier. But, like the flight of Apollo 13 some four decades later, the mundane was transformed into the sensational by a hair-raising accident.

After a couple of days, the weight of ice forming on the *Italia's* huge body brought the airship down low. Around half past ten in the morning, on May 25, the control cabin struck the icy surface of the Arctic Ocean and was ripped from the rest of the airship. Freed of the extra weight, the *Italia* rose into the air, carrying off six men inside the hull to their deaths.

The remains of the craft were never recovered, but one can imagine the frantic efforts of the six on board, fumbling with increasingly freezing fingers as the craft rose higher in the sky, in an attempt to release the hydrogen and get them back to the ice pack. Perhaps the airship crashed and its gas ignited because, somewhere away from the wreck of the control cabin, a column of smoke was seen rising into the sky.

Back on the ground, the men who had been in the cabin when it was torn off were in a desperate situation. One man had been killed, Nobile had broken an arm and a leg, and another man, Natal Cecioni, also had a broken leg. All the *Italia's* crew members were aeronauts, rather than explorers, and none of them had any experience of polar conditions. Their radio was broken, and there was little hope of rescue.

The men fell into acrimonious argument. Three of them, two Italians named Mariano and Zappi, and a Swedish scientist named Finn Malmgren, decided they would walk south through the ice, to try to reach help. The rest stayed with the shattered cabin, hoping their food supplies would last.

Soon after the three men set off south, the *Italia's* radio operator succeeded in fixing his set. An SOS was repeatedly transmitted to the *Città di Milano*. The message was picked up, but when the radio operator reported it to a senior officer, he was told to ignore it. Having lost both sight and radio contact with the *Italia*, the officer was convinced no one had survived and that the message must be referring to something else. But the *Italia* crew was not totally without luck. In Archangelsk, on the northern tip of Russia's western border, the message was picked up by a radio ham (an amateur radio enthusiast).

The radio ham alerted the Russian government in

Moscow, who, in turn, got in touch with the Italian government. Six nations took part in the search to rescue the crew of the *Italia*, and 18 ships, 22 planes and 1,500 men were sent out to comb the area where the crew reported they had crashed.

On June 18, 23 days after the crash, the cabin and a red tent erected by the men were spotted by a plane. The plane was not equipped to land on ice, so it flew low over the spot, to assure the survivors they had been seen. Five days later, after a lull caused by poor weather, a small plane landed on the ice next to them.

There was only room on the plane for one other person, and Nobile suggested they take Cecioni, who was the most badly injured. But this noble gesture went awry. The Swedish pilot argued with Nobile, suggesting it would be much better for him to come himself, so he could coordinate the rescue operation. Nobile was persuaded, and hopped aboard, together with his dog, Titina. This turned out to be a public relations disaster. The newspapers wasted no time in portraying Nobile as a coward who abandoned his men to escape with his dog. Mussolini, watching the whole debacle with mounting rage, demoted Nobile from his recently acquired rank of general. The trip had turned into a national humiliation.

While all this was going on, Nobile's old companion and now resentful enemy, Amundsen, had resolved to help with the rescue too. It's not clear whether his motive was to humiliate Nobile, or whether he was prompted by genuine concern for the stranded men. But his offer to help was certainly strange in the light of hostile comments he had made about Nobile in the autobiography he had recently published.

Mussolini, sensing further humiliation, told the Norwegian government in the strongest terms that Amundsen's help was not required. But, having offered his help, Amundsen felt obliged to go. So when the French provided him with a Latham 47 seaplane, together with a pilot and crew of three, he came aboard, bringing a friend with him. As the heavily loaded plane struggled north to the Arctic town of Tromsø, it became obvious that it was not up to the journey. But French and Norwegian national pride drove the men to continue. On June 18, the day the *Italia* survivors were spotted by a Swedish plane, the Latham took off from the northern coast of Norway, and was never seen again. Amundsen and the others vanished with it.

For the survivors of the *Italia*, freezing, starving, and thoroughly miserable, there was more torment to come. The day after the first plane landed and took Nobile away, it returned with only one pilot, intent on taking the men off two at a time. But, when the plane came down to land, it flipped over on the snow, and the pilot joined the wretched men waiting for rescue. Then, over the next few days, thick fog came down, making further flying impossible. But, as more flights were being planned, a magnificent Russian icebreaker, the *Krassin*, came to the rescue. Sent toward the spot found by the aircraft, the ship reached their camp on July 12, and picked up the hapless men.

Soon after Nobile's men had been rescued by the *Krassin*, a lookout plane from the icebreaker spotted the men who had set out on foot after the *Italia* had crashed. But there were no longer three of them, only two. When they were picked up, they revealed that Malmgren was dead. Bit by bit, a squalid story emerged. Malmgren had become too weak to walk, and had asked the others to carry on without him. This they had readily agreed to do, but they had also taken his food and some of his clothing. Gossip soon spread that the two Italians had murdered the Swede so they could eat him. This too did nothing for Italian national prestige.

Further tragedy followed. An Italian seaplane sent to help in the rescue crashed on the journey home, killing its crew of three. Finally, on August 31, some remains of the French seaplane carrying Amundsen were found in the sea. A float and a fuel tank had been lashed together to construct a makeshift raft. Whoever had survived the crash into the sea had made one desperate attempt to get back south alive. The cold had defeated them. Their raft was still afloat but, perhaps one by one, too numb to hold on to their precarious platform, they had fallen off and slipped under the icy sea.

Nobile, his disgrace complete, went to live in Russia. Then he moved to the United States, and later to Spain. He eventually died in 1978, at the age of 93.

Interlude

From 1928-1992

Once almost impossibly remote, the Arctic and Antarctic are now easily accessible. The North Pole can be reached by powerful icebreakers, by submarines and by ski planes. Weather stations drift across its frozen surface. At the South Pole, there is a permanent settlement, the Scott-Amundsen Base, where huge C-130 transport planes land and take off when weather permits. The continent has 42 coastal and inland research stations.

But, despite the everyday evidence of human habitation, the Poles have remained a challenge for adventurers. As the 20th century came to an end, explorers competed to reach or cross the Poles in the most dangerous, hair-raising fashions. Where once whole teams of men would work together to reach a Pole, now they set out in ones or twos. At first, these attempts were "supported", with supplies being dropped by plane, or left along the route by others. Once this had been achieved, it became necessary to set new challenges, and some polar enthusiasts attempted to reach the Poles "unsupported".

It seems extraordinary, but less than a century after the epic journeys of Amundsen, Peary, Shackleton and Scott, one man, with a sled full of supplies, can now cross the Arctic or Antarctic entirely unaided.

Hard times at the bottom of the world

Ranulph Fiennes and Mike Stroud's 2,170km (1,350 mile) trek across the Antarctic had barely begun when Stroud fell into a crevasse. The two British adventurers were using parachute-like sails to haul them and their sledloads of equipment across the Filchner Ice Shelf, on the opening stage of their journey.

It was Fiennes who first saw the dark blue maw of the crevasse loom before them. He immediately threw himself to the ground, sliding to a bruising halt just before he reached its lip. Stroud was not so quick. As he fumbled with his sail-release cord, he heard Fiennes shout an anguished, "*Noooooooooo…*", before the ground dropped away beneath him.

In a continent devoid of man-eating wildlife, crevasses offer the single greatest threat of violent death to an unwary explorer. They are often concealed by a thin coating of snow, like a trap door, and anyone who stumbles over one can find themselves plummeting into a dark and deep ice cavern.

Fiennes's thoughts turned to what he would say to Stroud's wife and children. But fortunately Stroud had not fallen far. He had swung against the crevasse's hard ice wall and banged his head, then grabbed an icy nub before his sled caught up with him, dragging him down. He had glimpsed the terrifying depth of the crevasse as he veered over the top, and was convinced he was now falling to his death. Luckily, though, he landed on a narrow platform of hardened snow, about 6m (20ft) down, right next to his sled. On either side of him, vertical blue walls plunged down into deepening shades of darkness. The bottom of the crevasse was too far below to be seen.

As Fiennes peered over the edge, Stroud managed to cry, feebly, "I'm OK." Getting him out would not be too difficult, but the 220kg (485lb) sled was too heavy to haul up. It carried essential supplies, so they had to retrieve it or their adventure would come to a premature end.

Every time Stroud moved, snow fell away from his precarious perch. When he tried to stand up, his foot went straight through the snow. Unbalanced, he fell forward. He stretched out an arm to stop his fall, but that too broke through the snow platform. By now, the shock of the fall was beginning to wear off, and Stroud felt sick with fear. Fiennes called down, reminding Stroud that he had their long rope on his sled, and needed to throw it up to the surface. But this entailed finding it first. As he leaned over to unzip the cover on the sled, it lurched away from him, and more snow and ice fell away. Fortunately, the rope was right at the front, and Stroud managed to get hold of it and throw it up to the top. As Fiennes caught it, more pieces of ice dislodged themselves, piercing the snow platform as they fell into the depths.

Stroud's basic instinct was to get out as quickly as possible, but the only way to get the sled up to the surface was to throw up the food and equipment it held, until it was light enough to haul to the top. Feeling more confident now he was attached to a rope anchored above him, Stroud began to lob up fuel bottles, food packages and other equipment, until the sled was empty and light enough to pull up. Only then could he climb up the side of the crevasse. Once on top, he lay panting in the snow, elated but haunted by his narrow brush with death.

Sir Ranulph Twisleton-Wykeham-Fiennes ("Ran" to his friends) and Dr. Mike Stroud were attempting the first unsupported crossing of the Antarctic. It was late November 1992. In the hundred or so days ahead of them, they hoped to walk, ski and sail to the South Pole, and then carry on down the Beardmore Glacier and Ross Ice Shelf to the Scott Base on the shores of the Ross Sea. Their motives for making such an epic journey were many. Stroud, aged 37, was a medical researcher specializing in nutrition, and a survival consultant for the Ministry of Defence. He planned to take careful records of the slow deterioration of their bodies as they battled against the appalling hardships to come. Fiennes, a former Eton schoolboy and SAS army officer, was an old-fashioned professional adventurer. At 48, he was beginning to wonder if he was too old for such punishing expeditions – but, as he said at the time, "[This] is my job. It's the way I make my income." Fiennes was following in the footsteps of Peary and Shackleton. A veteran of many a hair-raising trek to the world's most dangerous locations, including several previous polar expeditions, Fiennes made a living by writing books and giving talks about his exploits. On this particular trip, the two men also hoped to raise funds for research into multiple sclerosis – every mile they walked would make huge sums of money from sponsors.

Fiennes and Stroud had been on polar expeditions together five times before. Experience told them that, as they grew frailer and more exhausted, their resolve to continue would ebb away. It was almost inevitable in conditions of such extreme hardship. On one Arctic trip, Stroud – who had been finding it hard to keep up with Fiennes – became so desperate to stop that he fantasized about killing his partner. He imagined shooting Fiennes with the gun he carried in case they were attacked by a polar bear. In the cold light of day, such murderous grudges could be seen as useful insights into the irrational thought processes of exhausted men. Such was their trust and friendship that, after the journey was over, both men could talk freely about it without animosity. But now, as they slogged through the

Antarctic, their friendship was once again about to be tested to the limit.

Part of the success of their partnership lay in the confidence each man had in the other's strengths and abilities. The two men were roughly physically equal. True, Fiennes was much taller, and also stronger, than Stroud, but he was 11 years older, and perhaps less resilient. Fiennes was a skilled navigator, with a wealth of experience and an iron determination. Stroud had an expert knowledge of the human body under stress. Both men admired the other's drive and resilience. But, as Fiennes pointed out in his account of the trip: "*If two saintly monks were to manhaul heavy loads, whilst increasingly deprived of food and subjected to mounting discomforts, they might maintain at least an outward show of mutual tolerance. If so, they would be the exception to the rule.*"

Early on, two decisions were made that would cause them dreadful hardship later in the journey. In an effort to save weight, when progress was good and the weather was mild, the two discarded rations and extra layers of warm clothing. But all too soon the wear and tear on their bodies – caused by an unholy combination of pulling heavy weights, trudging through sludgy snow, enduring the fierce ultraviolet rays of the Antarctic sun, and suffering from intense cold and fierce winds – caught up with them.

Their feet were especially vulnerable. Frostbite in their toes and fingers brought acute agony. Rubbing sores on their heels turned into blisters, which turned into festering ulcers. Halfway to the Pole, Stroud had to perform an exquisitely painful operation on his own foot, taking a scalpel to an infected abscess and draining it. They carried antibiotics to help treat such problems, but these often gave the men acute digestive trouble. In a howling gale, both would suffer the agony of churning guts for hours, until they could stand it no longer and have to unbutton their padded overalls, and squat down in the snow. Doing this, in the open, chilled their bodies to the core and carried a further risk of frostbite.

The thermos flask they used to carry their lunchtime soup soon became contaminated, inflicting additional torment on their tortured intestines. As well as being deeply unpleasant to cope with, this also meant their bodies were not digesting their limited rations properly. As the journey progressed, both men lost a third of their weight. First, their ravenous bodies used up any excess fat, which otherwise acted as insulation against the fierce cold. Then, their digestive systems began to eat into their muscles. By the time the men reached the South Pole, Stroud calculated that, on the days they walked, they were burning up 8,000 calories, but only eating 5,500.

Fiennes and Stroud were not the only people wanting to attempt an unsupporting crossing. They had a self-declared rival. At the same time as the two

British explorers were making their trip, a Norwegian named Erling Kagge had announced his intention to make the first unsupported journey alone to the Pole. The newspapers had turned this into a race. Fiennes and Stroud argued crabbily over whether or not they should reveal their own position to Kagge. To do so would be useful to the Norwegian, but not to do so would acknowledge that they felt a competitive rivalry with Kagge, which they were both uneasy about. Fiennes told Stroud that, "as expedition leader", he did not wish Kagge to know where they were. Stroud deeply resented this rank pulling – it did, after all, seem rather pompous on a two-man expedition. His festering anger turned into a blazing argument the next day, when Fiennes lagged behind him considerably as they trudged through the snow.

"I'm going as fast as I can," said Fiennes, "and I don't expect some little runt to tell me it's too slow."

Most of the journey was being made on foot, as it was often too windy, bumpy or dangerous because of crevasses to use the para-sails. Walking further drained Fiennes and Stroud's waning physical strength, and added greatly to their foot blisters and ulcers, although it did at least keep them warm. When they were able to make use of the sails, it was much quicker and used less of their energy. But because they did not have to work so hard, it was uncomfortably cold, and the sail harnesses also chafed, causing injuries to their shoulders and backs.

Christmas Day, which fell a few days before they reached the Pole, was a low point. As the two drank glutinous, luke-warm soup – which they never managed to keep hot enough to make its energy-giving high-fat content palatable – they both reflected glumly on what their own families would be eating. Fiennes presented Stroud with a huge chocolate bar as a present. Stroud, both touched and surprised by this generous gesture, wolfed it down, but also felt guilty that he had not thought to bring anything to give Fiennes.

At this stage of the journey the two men began to realize they had underestimated how much food they would need to consume. Their daily rations weren't giving them enough energy for the demands of the trip. Perpetually hungry, their bodies were breaking down their reserves of fat, and this process was producing chemicals called ketones, which make people feel both ill and depressed.

Stroud, especially, began to fantasize about faking an illness, such as a stroke, which would be serious enough to make Fiennes call off the expedition. Fiennes was despondent too, but his circumstances were different from Stroud's. As leader of the expedition, he was liable for the cost of any air rescue. He was also in serious financial trouble. Unwise investments had left him with massive debts, and, understandably, he had every reason both for wanting to finish the expedition and for avoiding additional costs.

54 days into the trip, Stroud had another bout of serious digestive trouble. Too weak to continue, he told Fiennes he had to stop to rest for a few hours. He was surprised and hurt to discover that Fiennes was actually angry with him. The two men put up their tent in strained silence. Then Stroud took some medicine and slept for several hours. He woke feeling much better, but was astonished to hear Fiennes tell him that he had decided to continue the journey alone once they'd reached the Pole.

"This is the second time we've had to stop for you," Fiennes said. "If you can't take it, I'm not going to wait for you."

Fiennes went on to say they were close enough now to be certain of reaching the Pole and, when they got there, Stroud could take a plane out with minimal expense.

Stroud was astounded, and very angry. His response seemed to shake Fiennes out of his plan. Fiennes looked ashamed, and apologized. After weeks of feeling weak, he explained, he had suddenly had a second wind. He had been unreasonably frustrated at being held back by Stroud's stomach problems.

Later, Stroud sat fuming in the tent, writing his journal. Fiennes turned to him and said, in a rare display of affection, "Mike, you're a real brick."

Just at that moment, Stroud was writing: "*Ran is a real ★★★★★*" in his journal. The journey was not halfway over, and they were in danger of seriously falling out. Yet despite their occasional arguments, both men were well aware of how their physical deterioration was contributing to their bad tempers. This enabled them to keep on good terms for most of the time.

68 days into the trip, they reached the South Pole. Here, at the Pole itself – marked, in a rather tongue-in-cheek fashion, by a large, silver bauble placed on a striped barber's pole – they met a party of American women who had walked to the Pole. It was a great joy for Fiennes and Stroud to meet and talk to other people. They set up their tent and offered tea to their new friends. Seeing their filthy, porridge-encrusted cups, the women declined, but they sat together happily, swapping stories.

Close to the Pole lay piles of packaging and spent fuel containers. There were also research and accommodation buildings, complete with all the trappings of a comfortable life: showers, hot food, books and company – all the things they longed for. But the South Pole base has a policy of not supporting independent adventurers (such expeditions, they feel, are dangerous and should not be encouraged, although they are always prepared to assist and rescue in an emergency). Besides, this was an "unsupported" attempt, and that meant no help in any way from anyone. Stroud, especially, felt quite tearful as they packed up their tent and walked away from this oasis of human habitation.

Soon after their brief stop at the Pole, they encountered a strange and unsettling phenomenon. Walking over an area of thin, flat ice, they would often plunge 15cm (6 inches) down to another layer beneath. It was unsettling, because it felt like the start of a fall into a crevasse. Sometimes, triggered by their footsteps, the ice in a large area around them would break up and drop down to the layer below. When this happened, it made a colossal noise, like a jet plane approaching.

Fiennes and Stroud plodded on through a stretch of their journey that seemed to be permanently uphill. They were demoralized to hear that, when news of their reaching the Pole had been announced, they had been mocked by a couple of British newspapers. Articles had put forward the idea that, with modern clothing, equipment and communications, polar exploration was now all too easy, belittling the suffering they had been through. Both men felt indignant about this. It was true that their sleds were made of a combination of metal and plastics, making them lighter and stronger than Scott and Shackleton's wooden ones, but the men were probably just as hungry and exhausted as their predecessors. Their synthetic-fabric clothing might have been lighter than the furs and natural fabrics worn earlier in the century, but these modern clothes were not necessarily warmer.

Their one indisputable advantage was that they carried the latest hi-tech navigation aids. Although their satellite locator device would frequently bleep and whirr for several minutes before declaring "ERROR", and have to be reset, when it did work, it gave them their exact position. Both men, though, were wounded by the common misconception that, if disaster struck, they could be rescued in a flash. True, they could summon help. But, if the weather was bad, they might have to wait a week or more before a plane could fly out to look for them. Besides, as Mike Stroud had already discovered, a crevasse could claim him just as easily as it could a Scott, Wilson or Oates.

The second half of the journey was possibly even worse than the first. As January passed, the coming Antarctic winter began to take a hold. As colder, stormier weather became more frequent, their chances of a prompt emergency air rescue also became more unlikely. Fiennes's foot grew worse, but he gritted his teeth and tried to forget this nagging pain. Stroud lost both his ski sticks, so Fiennes generously gave him one of his.

Then, 81 days into the journey, Stroud, already weakened, fell and fractured his ankle, adding greatly to the pain he felt in his feet. This additional handicap led to arguments with Fiennes. It might seem heartless to berate a man with a damaged ankle for not keeping up, especially as Stroud had led the way for much of the journey. Yet Fiennes's frustration was understandable. Stopping for up to 10 minutes to allow Stroud to catch up, Fiennes would be literally freezing to death by the time he could begin walking again and start to feel warmer.

By now, both men were bags of bones. Stroud noted: "*My bed is getting bonier every night*". When they rested, sleep was difficult to find. Frost-bitten hands and feet, frozen numb during the day, would thaw and ache, painfully and insistently. Stroud's hands were so raw that he could not bear the thought of taking his gloves on and off. Fiennes had such a badly frost-bitten left foot that his toes had merged into one grotesque, black, fluid-filled bag, from which oozed a repulsive, stinking liquid. Afterwards he wrote that, when his feet were like that, he would rather have been tortured by the Gestapo (the Nazi secret police) than have to put on his boots.

Nonetheless, they battled on through the Beardmore Glacier. Now starvation began to take hold, and both men fantasized wildly about food. Each night in the tent, each would eye the other warily, to make sure neither got a mouthful more than the other – a situation that could easily have led to more arguments. But, in a commendable display of manners and courtesy, they took turns in strict rotation, to lick the spoon and mug of every last scrap of food.

On day 91, shortly after Fiennes had fallen up to his chest through a snow-covered crevasse, they eventually reached the Ross Ice Shelf. Now they could claim to have crossed the Antarctic continent.

But the ocean itself, beyond this stretch of sea ice, was still 580km (360 miles) further north. They pressed on, intending to complete their route to the Scott Base. But then Stroud began to suffer from delirium, the effect of severe hypothermia, and Fiennes's rotting, frost-bitten feet were causing him constant agony. It was time to call it a day. They were 96 days into their trip, and only 400km (250 miles) short of their final intended destination.

Fiennes set up their tent and called up a rescue plane on his radio. They were lucky with the weather and were told to expect to be picked within a few hours. Now their supplies no longer needed to last, they ate like there was no tomorrow. Waiting for their plane, Stroud ate 12 chocolate bars in three hours.

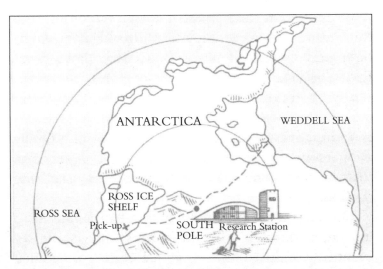

This map shows the journey made by Fiennes and Stroud.

Afterwards, Fiennes reckoned that, had they continued, they would both have died somewhere on the Ross Ice Shelf. In the days that followed, their bodies succumbed to extreme exhaustion. Their limbs swelled to grotesque proportions, and they had to be helped on and off planes. When they didn't sleep, they ate. Back in England, in the weeks after his return, Fiennes would have muesli, sugar puffs, toast and eggs for breakfast, and then eat five doughnuts with coffee an hour later.

Both Fiennes and Stroud wrote books about their extraordinary adventure. Neither made any secret of their animosities and arguments. These accounts leave readers in no doubt that both men felt considerable anger towards the other at certain times during the journey, though there is also a deep sense of regret at the way they behaved with each other. But explorers have argued their way across both frozen Poles. Even that most amiable and likeable explorer, Sir Ernest Shackleton, threatened Captain Robert Scott with violence, and once hit a crewmate until he did as he was told. Stroud and Fiennes were immensely courageous in their determination to carry on through extreme suffering. Perhaps it's surprising they didn't quarrel more.

Stroud and Fiennes both finish their books on a conciliatory note. Stroud writes that some of Fiennes's conduct "*made me spit*". But he also said that he would gladly go with him on another expedition.

Fiennes might have compared Stroud to "*a crotchety old woman*", but he also spoke openly of his admiration for his colleague, and quoted Captain Oates: "*when a man is having a hard time he says hard things about other people which he would regret afterwards.*" Today, the two men are still good friends and, since their Antarctic expedition, have made another trip together in the Canadian Rockies.

Been there,
done that...

At the dawn of the 21st century, the polar regions
had little left to offer the world's elite band of
professional adventurers. Interviewed in the literary
magazine *January*, in October, 2001, Sir Ranulph
Fiennes was asked if he would visit the Poles again.
He sighed and said regretfully, "I'm not planning
polar expeditions because they've all been done;
every single one of them has been done... the only
[challenges] left are gimmicky: you have to go by
camel or motorbike or something to be first. So the
genuine firsts – supported and unsupported – are all
now done."

The taker of many of these records is an ex-
Norwegian Army commando and deep-sea diver
named Børge Ousland. Now a professional guide
who takes tourists on planes to the North Pole, he
managed to accomplish with ease polar feats which
would leave his early 20th-century predecessors
open-mouthed with astonishment. But it was not all
plain sailing. To do what Ousland did still required a
character every bit as courageous and determined as
those who came before him.

Ousland's first serious bid for polar fame occurred

in 1990, when he set off with Geir Randby and Erling Kagge from Ward Hunt Island, on the north coast of Ellesmere Island, on an unsupported trip to the North Pole. Nine days into the journey, Randby injured his back and a plane was called to fetch him. Despite successfully reaching the Pole, Ousland and Kagge found their achievement was not accepted by many fellow adventurers, as they had had some help – the airlift of their injured colleague.

Ousland settled the matter spectacularly when he set off on his own from Cape Arktichesky, Severnaya Zemlya, on March 2, 1994. Starting each day before dawn, his heavy sled tied behind him, he would head through the fractured ice of the Arctic Ocean. Alone in a vast white canvas, the only sound he would usually hear would be the squeaking of his sled on the ice, his own muffled breathing, or the howl of the polar wind. In the first days of his journey, he was particularly struck by the beauty of his surroundings. The clear, frosty air and sunshine on the ice, snow and water create a special kind of light unique to the North Pole.

As the journey progressed, Ousland established a rhythm: one and a half hours walking, then a rest for food and water. Despite the extreme cold, which caused icicles to form in his beard and pearls of frost to line his eyelashes, he felt warm enough in his bright red waterproof overalls. Sometimes, his path was impeded by enormous leads (gaps in the ice), and his journey became like a foray through a giant maze, with endless detours to find a safe way through. But Ousland's strength and luck held. By April 22, he had reached the Pole – the first successful, unsupported solo attempt.

Over in the Antarctic, the final challenges were also falling fast. In 1993, Ousland's Arctic colleague Erling Kagge had made the first unsupported solo journey to the South Pole (see also page 120). With time and opportunity running out, Ousland decided to try for an unsupported solo crossing. His first attempt, in 1995, ended in frostbite and failure, but he was back within a year. On his 1996 journey, he faced stiff competition from two other polar adventurers – Ranulph Fiennes and a Polish explorer, Marek Kaminski. Both were intending to do the same thing – although in the end they proved to be no competition at all. Fiennes fell victim to kidney stones and had to be evacuated, and Kaminski injured himself in an accident and stopped once he had reached the Pole.

Ousland set out on skis from Berkner Island on the Weddell Sea on November 15, with a 180kg (400lb) sled and a parachute-like sail. The sail was a phenomenal success. With a smooth surface and a good wind, he once covered 226km (140 miles) in a single day. But Ousland had to keep his senses about him. Temperatures dropped as low as -55°C (-67°F) and, when the weather was bad, the sky seemed to be enveloped in a sheet of white. There was no horizon and forward visibility was severely limited. Ahead lay crevasses and fragile snow bridges, which Ousland called "potential trap-doors into the abyss". It would be all too easy to fall in and vanish forever.

But on good days the sun shone, bringing a frosty glow to the strangely stark landscape. Much of Ousland's success lay in his positive attitude. He decided from the start that he would try to seek as much beauty as he could from his surroundings. "*I had two alternatives,*" he wrote. "*I could look about me and say that it was white, deserted, exhausting and wretchedly dull. Or I could invert it into something new and positive; seek out the beauty in nature, the changes in light, shapes and colours.*" As he trudged along, he listened to music. His personal stereo played a selection of songs by Jimi Hendrix, ZZ Top and Tom Petty: driving, strutting rock, or "something that will keep you going", as Ousland described it. Good days like this filled him with euphoria.

He reached the South Pole on December 19. Here were the white domes and buildings of the Amundsen-Scott Station. He knew, of course, that the station was famous for giving a frosty reception to adventurers like himself. This suited him down to the ground. He was desperate for human company, warmth, a shower and other ordinary 20th-century creature comforts. His diet of freeze-dried meat, porridge and other basic foods was boring him intensely. But he knew if any hospitality was offered to him, he might decide then and there to end his journey. He would also no longer be able to claim he had made an unsupported trip.

From the Pole, he followed Amundsen's route down the Axel Heiberg Glacier. During this section of his journey, Christmas Day fell. The weather had closed in around him, with storms and gales shaking his tent. But he was determined to make Christmas special. Well-prepared, he had brought a traditional Norwegian Christmas dinner: smoked and salted lamb, and a small almond cake. He had even brought presents and cards with him, carefully stashed in his sled.

Then, he crossed over the Ross Ice Shelf and headed for the Scott Base at McMurdo Sound. As he approached the end of his journey, the sun shone benignly, and a gentle breeze blew towards him. Around 20km (12 miles) from the end, he realized he could smell the sea. Then, he saw a speck on the horizon – a plane was taking off from the airbase there. The nearer he got, the more he became aware of human activity: there was a whiff of exhaust, and the hum of generators, and then buildings came into view.

Ousland wondered what sort of reception he would get from the people on the base. As he walked across the airfield, he came upon a mechanic working on a fire engine. The man looked up, then just ignored him. After all the isolation of his journey, Ousland felt crushed.

"You are the first person I have seen since the South Pole," he told him.

Now the mechanic looked astounded. It was January 17, 1997. Ousland's astonishing 2,840km (1,775 mile) journey had taken him only 64 days.

Other Arctic records came and went. In February 2000, two Norwegians, Rune Gjeldnes and Toré Larsen, made a complete, unsupported crossing of the Arctic Ocean via the North Pole. There was only one more record left to break – unsupported and solo – and it was Børge Ousland who was determined to do it. Starting off again at Cape Arktichesky on March 3, 2001, he stood on its barren, wind-battered cliffs, staring at the forbidding Arctic Ocean. Right by the coast, huge chunks of ice crashed into each other, tossed by titanic currents and winds. In areas where ice had packed together, the ocean would open and close into huge leads, almost as if it had a life of its own.

Ousland set out, retracing the steps he'd taken seven years previously. For this journey, he took an inflatable drysuit, to allow him to cross open leads in the ice. Especially designed for lethally cold water, the watertight suit kept a layer of air between the wearer and the water, both protecting him from the cold and allowing him to float easily, dragging his supplies behind him. As ever, Ousland's equipment was carefully chosen. His sled contained 166kg (365lb) of food and fuel. He carried a mobile phone, a Global Positioning System (GPS) satellite navigation device, and a sail. On a good day, he could sail through the ice for maybe ten hours. But the sail also spelled potential disaster. At speed, a fall could mean a broken arm or leg and an abrupt end to his journey.

Right from the start, Ousland knew he was facing a terrible ordeal. He described his skiing, walking and swimming journey as "a triathlon from hell". Before him lay 1,996km (1,240 miles) of broken ice and water. The Arctic, he recalled, was so much more forbidding than the Antarctic, because you were never on solid ground. On ice, he could never be entirely certain of his surroundings, and knew that he could fall through into freezing water at any point.

Almost at once, he encountered a problem that was so basic he felt embarrassed about it. That night, as he made camp and began to prepare an evening meal, he realized there was no fresh water to drink or cook with. He was surrounded by frozen water, but it was *seawater*, so all of it was salty. Ousland had expected to find snow, which when melted becomes fresh water, but none had fallen for several days. He retired to his tent that night with a raging thirst, knowing he had to find drinking water the next morning.

During the dead of night, he was woken by the terrifying sound of moving sea ice. All around him, the ice piled high in layers around his camp site, grinding and cracking as floe piled upon floe.

Expecting to be crushed at any moment, Ousland piled all his essentials, his emergency beacon and cooking equipment into his sleeping bag. As the ice edged closer, he thought he would have to pick up his belongings and run. But, as day began to break, the moving ice subsided, and an eerie calm descended on the camp site.

With darkness fading, Ousland could see that his entire surroundings had changed. Only a space around his camp site, about 10 x 15m (30 x 50ft), remained untouched. His luck held, for in the bright morning light he could see ice crystals glistening on the surrounding ice blocks. He tasted them, and was delighted to discover they were pure water. He spent an hour gingerly collecting the frozen morning dew, until he had enough to fill a cooking pot.

For the next week, Ousland battled through compacted walls of iron-hard ice. It was heavy going and exhausting work. Battered by the rough terrain, his sled cracked. He tried to repair it, drilling 262 holes in the side and sewing the cracks together, but his best efforts failed. There was nothing to do but call for assistance. A new sled arrived by helicopter. Watching the helicopter prepare to take off was one of the worst moments of the trip. Ousland desperately wanted to join the crew and return to warmth and human company. It was several days before his resolve and morale returned to normal.

But, amid all the struggle, there was still time to

admire his harsh environment. As evening fell, the sky turned from deep blue to black. In the clear polar air, the stars came out to twinkle with an unaccustomed brightness. As night fell, a frosty mist rose from surrounding leads of dark water. When the Northern Lights played in the night sky, the whole scene had an unreal, hallucinogenic magic about it.

Ousland battled on through fierce winds and fractured ice, finally arriving at the Pole on April 23. After six weeks alone, he was confronted by the sight of a party of tourists flown in for the day, including an Arab man dressed, rather incongruously, in full national costume. The tour leaders, two esteemed polar explorers named Mikhail Malakhov and Richard Weber, offered him a warming meal of chilli con carne, which Ousland was delighted to accept.

Reaching the Pole meant Ousland was more than halfway through his journey, for it lies approximately three-fifths of the way between Severnaya Zemlya and his destination, Ellesmere Island. The rest of the journey went smoothly enough. Ousland reached Ward Hunt Island, just off the north coast of Ellesmere Island, on May 23. He had covered 1,996km (1,250 miles) in just 82 days. Waiting to greet him with a bottle of champagne were his girlfriend and his mother, forewarned by mobile phone. Ousland was fit and well, but he had lost around 23kg (50lb) in weight. He might have had a little help along the way, but he had succeeded in completing a remarkable solo journey.

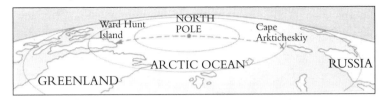

This map shows Ousland's trans-Arctic crossing of 2001, from Cape Arkticheskiy to Ward Hunt Island.

Today, it really does seem that there are no more genuine "firsts" left for the Poles – and, until someone walks there backwards with their eyes shut, or stark naked and carrying a giant panda, it is difficult to imagine the world's media taking much of an interest in any further polar adventures.

Fantastic leaps in technology over the last century mean that it is no longer remarkable for human beings to explore these once forbidding, bleak and beautiful places. Dependable air travel can now place people at either Pole, and radio communication can keep them in touch with the outside world. At the South Pole, buildings made of strong, lightweight materials enable researchers to live in a reasonable degree of comfort and security. But, despite this, the Poles are still the same unforgiving, lethally hostile environments they always were. All of which makes the courage and determination of the explorers and adventurers who have risked their lives to go there all the more extraordinary.

Glossary

This glossary explains some of the specialized words used in this book. Words which appear in *italics* are defined elsewhere in the glossary.

Antarctica *Also known as the* **Antarctic**. Huge frozen continent at the bottom of the world.

Antarctic circle An imaginary circle around the earth on a map, at *latitude* 66° south.

Arctic Huge frozen ocean at the top of the world.

Arctic circle An imaginary circle around the earth on a map, at *latitude* 66° north.

Aurora australis *Also known as the* **Southern Lights**. Bands of green, red or yellow light seen in the sky in the *Antarctic*.

Aurora borealis *Also known as the* **Northern Lights**. Bands of green, red or yellow light seen in the sky in the *Arctic*.

Blizzard An extreme snowstorm.

Chronometer A timepiece designed to be extremely accurate, and used as a navigation instrument at sea.

Crevasse A deep crack or hole in thick ice, especially in a glacier.

Eskimo An old-fashioned word for the people who live in the *Arctic*.

Frostbite A dangerous medical condition where parts of the body become frozen and can be irreparably damaged.

Glacier A large river of ice, usually flowing down from a mountain.

Iceberg A large chunk of ice floating in the sea, which has broken away from a glacier or iceshelf.

Ice cap A huge layer of very thick ice, which covers a vast landmass, such as Greenland or *Antarctica*.

Ice floe A free-floating block of flat ice in the sea.

Ice shelf A layer of thick ice attached to a large bay.

Inuit Modern name for people who live in the Northern Polar region, especially the native

Glossary

people of Canada and Greenland.
Inuit is used for the plural, and
Inuk for the singular.

Kayak A small *Inuit* canoe
made from animal bones and
skin.

Latitude Horizontal lines on a
map which divide the world. The
North Pole is at latitude 90° north
and the *South Pole* is at latitude
90° south.

Longitude Vertical lines on a
map which divide the world. All
lines of longitude meet up at the
North and *South Poles*.

Manhauling Pulling sleds
without the aid of animals or
windpower.

North Pole The northernmost
point on earth.

Northeast passage A route
from Europe to China and Japan,
via the north coast of Russia.

Northern Lights *See Aurora
Borealis.*

Northwest passage A route
from Europe to China and Japan,
via the north coast of North
America.

Pemmican Dried meat or fish
mixed with fat, vegetables and
cereals to make a highly
nutritious, hard, cake-like bar.

Scurvy A disease caused by lack
of Vitamin C, with symptoms
including extreme fatigue,
bleeding and ulcers.

South Pole The southernmost
point on earth.

Southern Lights *See Aurora
Australis.*

Specimen An item collected
for the purpose of medical or
scientific study.

Supported crossing In the
sense used in this book, a journey
across either Pole, undertaken
with assistance, for example, food
being left en route by plane.

Unsupported crossing In the
sense used in this book, a journey
across either Pole, undertaken
without any assistance.

Also from Usborne True Stories

TRUE STORIES OF
HEROES

PAUL DOWSWELL

His blood ran cold and Perevozchenko
was seized by panic. He knew that his
body was absorbing lethal doses of
radiation, but instead of fleeing he
stayed to search for his colleague.
Peering into the dark through a
broken window that overlooked the
reactor hall, he could see only a mass
of tangled wreckage.

By now he had absorbed so much
radiation he felt as if his whole body
was on fire. But then he remembered
that there were several other men near
to the explosion who might also be
trapped . . .

From firefighters battling with a blazing nuclear
reactor to a helicopter rescue team on board a fast-
sinking ship, this is an amazingly vivid collection of
stories about men and women whose extraordinary
courage has captured the imagination of millions.